Differentiating Instruction With Menus

for the Inclusive Classroom

Math

Differentiating Instruction With Menus

for the Inclusive Classroom

Math

Laurie E. Westphal

PRUFROCK PRESS INC.
WACO, TEXAS

Library of Congress Cataloging-in-Publication Data

Westphal, Laurie E., 1967-
 Differentiating instruction with menus for the inclusive classroom. Math, grades K-2 / by Laurie E. Westphal.
    pages cm
 Includes bibliographical references.
 ISBN 978-1-61821-032-6 (pbk.)
 1. Mathematics--Study and teaching (Primary) 2. Mathematics--Study and teaching (Early childhood) 3. Individualized instruction.
 4. Inclusive education. I. Title.
 QA135.6.W4742 2013
 372.7--dc23
                            2012039527

Edited by Jennifer Robins

Production design by Raquel Trevino

ISBN-13: 978-1-61821-032-6

At the time of this book's publication, all facts and figures cited are the most current available; all telephone numbers, addresses, and website URLs are accurate and active; all publications, organizations, websites, and other resources exist as described in this book; and all have been verified. The author and Prufrock Press make no warranty or guarantee concerning the information and materials given out by organizations or content found at websites, and we are not responsible for any changes that occur after this book's publication. If you find an error or believe that a resource listed here is not as described, please contact Prufrock Press.

Prufrock Press Inc.
P.O. Box 8813
Waco, TX 76714-8813
Phone: (800) 998-2208
Fax: (800) 240-0333
http://www.prufrock.com

CONTENTS

Author's Note

If you are familiar with books on various differentiation strategies, then you probably know about my Differentiating Instruction With Menus series, and you may be wondering about the differences between that series and this one, the Differentiating Instruction With Menus for the Inclusive Classroom series. In fact, when we first discussed creating this series, my editor asked how we could avoid having one series "cannibalize" (graphic, but a great word!) the other. Well, here is how I envision the two series being used:

These two series stand on their own if:
- You teach mostly lower ability, on-level, and ESL students and would like to modify your lessons on your own to accommodate a few advanced students. In this case, use this series, Differentiating Instruction With Menus for the Inclusive Classroom.
- You teach mostly advanced and high-ability students and would like to modify your lessons on your own to accommodate a few lower level students. In this case, use the Differentiating Instruction With Menus series.

These two series can serve as companions to one another if:
- You teach students with a wide range of abilities (from special education to gifted) and would benefit from having a total of three menus for a given topic of study: those for lower ability and on-level students (provided by this series, Differentiating Instruction With Menus for the Inclusive Classroom) and those for high-ability students (provided by the Differentiating Instruction With Menus series).

The menu designs used in this book reflect a successful modification technique I began using in my own classroom as the range of my students' ability levels widened. I experimented with many ways to use menus, from having students of all ability levels work on the same menu with the same expectations, to having everyone work on the same menu with modified contracted expectations, to using leveled menus where each student received one of three menus with some overlapping activities based on readiness, abilities, or preassessment results. I found that if the students in a given classroom had similar ability levels, I could use one menu with every student with slight modifications; however, the greater the span of ability levels, the more I needed the different leveled menus to reach everyone. Each book in the Differentiating Instruction With Menus for the Inclusive Classroom series has two leveled menus for the objectives covered: a lower level menu indicated by a ▲ and an on-level menu indicated by a ●. This way, teachers can provide more options to students with diverse abilities in the inclusive classroom. If used with the corresponding book in the Differentiating Instruction With Menus series, the teacher has a total of three leveled menus to work with.

Many teachers have told me how helpful the original Differentiating Instruction With Menus books are and how they have modified the books' menus to meet the needs of their lower level students. Teachers are always the first to make adjustments and find solutions, but wouldn't it be great if they had these preparations and changes already made for them? This is the purpose of the Differentiating Instruction With Menus for the Inclusive Classroom series.

—Laurie E. Westphal

CHAPTER 1

Choice in the Inclusive Primary Classroom

"So, I can do as many as I want? Really?" stuttered one of my second-grade students as he looked, surprised, from the paper in his hand to me. I had just handed out a Getting to Know You Pick 3 menu and explained to the small-group members that they would need to complete at least three choices from the list in order to share a few things about themselves with the group and me.

Let's begin by addressing the concept of the inclusive classroom. The term *inclusive* (vs. exclusive) leads one to believe that we are discussing a situation in which all students are included. In the simplest of terms, that is exactly what we are referring to as an inclusive classroom: a classroom that may have special needs students, on-level students, bilingual or ESL students, and gifted students. Although the concept is a simple one, the considerations are significant.

When thinking about the inclusive classroom and its unique ambiance, one must first consider the needs of the range of students within the classroom. Mercer, Lane, Jordan, Allsopp, and Eisele (1996) stated it best in their assessment of the needs in an inclusive classroom:

> Students who are academically gifted, those who have had abundant experiences, and those who have demonstrated

proficiency with lesson content typically tend to perform well when instruction is anchored at the "implicit" end of the instructional continuum. In contrast, low-performing students (i.e., students at risk for school failure, students with learning disabilities, and students with other special needs) and students with limited experience or proficiency with lesson content are most successful when instruction is explicit. Students with average academic performance tend to benefit most from the use of a variety of instructional methods that address individual needs. Instructional decisions for most students, therefore, should be based on assessment of individual needs. (pp. 230–231)

Acknowledging these varied and often contradictory needs that arise within an inclusive classroom can lead to frustration when trying to make one assignment or task fit everyone's needs. There are few—if any—traditional, teacher-directed lessons that can be implicit, explicit, and based on individual needs all at the same time. There is, however, one technique that tries to accomplish this: choice.

CHOICE: THE SUPERMAN OF TECHNIQUES?

Can the offering of appropriate choices really be the hero of the inclusive classroom? Can it leap buildings in a single bound and meet the needs of our implicit, explicit, and individual interests? Yes! By considering the use and benefits of choice, we can see that by offering choices, teachers really can meet the needs of the whole range of students in a primary inclusive classroom. Ask adults whether they would prefer to choose what to do or be told what to do, and of course, they will say they would prefer to have a choice. Students have the same feelings. Although they may not be experienced in making choices, they will make choices based on their needs, just as adults do—which makes everyone involved in the inclusive experience a little less stressed and frustrated.

PRIMARY STUDENTS AND CHOICE

"I think it is the best one because I like it."

—Kindergarten student, when asked to defend his activity of choice

Choice can be frustrating for both the teacher (who is trying to draw the best from his or her young students) and the students (who are trying to do what the teacher is asking, but are just not sure how to do it). Choice and independent thinking on a higher level are developmental in nature, as well as cognitive skills. When given a choice between tools to complete a product, most primary students have not yet developed their higher level thinking skills enough to respond with a well-thought-out, analytical response. Instead, a 5-year-old may defend or evaluate his choice by stating that it was the one he liked or that it was red, his favorite color. Does that imply that primary students are not capable of making choices or processing at the analysis level or higher? Definitely not! Primary students are very capable of making choices and enjoy doing so with some guidance. This guidance comes in minimizing the number of choices a student faces at once, as well as assisting in the choice process.

MAKING GOOD CHOICES IS A SKILL

"I wanted you to know, I never thought of [making good choices as a skill] that way. That really opened my eyes."

—Kindergarten teacher

When we think of making good choices as a skill, much like writing an effective paragraph, it becomes easy enough to understand the processes needed to encourage primary students to make their own choices. In keeping with this analogy, children could certainly figure out how to write on their own, perhaps even how to compose sentences and paragraphs by using other examples as models. Imagine, however, the progress and strength of the writing produced when children are given guidance and even the most basic of instruction on how to accomplish this task. The written piece is still their own, but the quality of the finished piece is much stronger when guidance is given during the process. The same is true with the quality of choices children can make in the classroom.

As with writing, students—especially those with special needs—can make choices on their own, but when the teacher provides background knowledge and assistance, those choices become more meaningful, and the products become richer. Although all students certainly need guidance, primary students will need the most; they often have not been in an educational setting long enough to have experienced different products, and the idea of choice is usually new to them. Some children may have experienced choice only when their parents allowed them to choose between different outfits or breakfast options for the day. Some may not have experienced even this level of choice. This can cause frustration for both the teacher and the student.

TEACHING CHOICES AS A SKILL

"When it comes to choice, some of my students just aren't receptive."

—First-grade teacher

So, what is the best way to provide this guidance and develop students' skill of making good choices? First, choose the appropriate number of options for your students. Although the goal might be to have students choose between nine different options, teachers should start by having their students choose between three predetermined choices the first day (if they were using a Three-Shape menu, students might choose one circle activity from the row of three circles). Then, after those products have been created, students can choose between another set of three options a few days later and perhaps another three the following week. By breaking down students' choices, teachers are reinforcing how to approach a more complex and/or varied choice format in the future. Primary students—even kindergarten students—can work up to making complex choices from longer lists of options as their choice skill level increases.

"My first menu bombed. I had given it out to the students, told them to pick what they wanted to do, [and given them] the deadline at the end of the week. Students either bugged me all week with questions or they didn't do anything. . . . The second one went so much better. I did a build-up with lots of excitement and guidance for each choice. My students did a great job! Some even did more than the minimum!"

—Second-grade teacher

Second, students will need guidance on how to select the options that are right for them. They may not automatically gravitate toward options without an exciting and detailed description of each choice. For the most part, primary students are still in the "pleasing the teacher" phase, which means that when given a choice, they will usually choose what they think will make the teacher happy. This means that when the teacher discusses the different menu options, the teacher has to be equally as excited about all of them. The discussion of the different choices has to be animated and specific. For example, if the content is all very similar, the focus would be on the product: "If you want to do some singing, this one is for you!" or "If you want to write and draw, circle this one as a maybe!" Sometimes, choices may differ based on both content and product, in which case both can be pointed out to students to assist them in making good choices for themselves: "You have some different choices in our Earth science unit. If you want to do something with dinosaurs and drawing, circle this one as a maybe. If you are thinking you want to do something with collecting rocks, this one might be for you." Primary students, although egocentric in nature, have not yet pondered who they really are and often have trouble choosing between product types and content on their own. The more exposure they have to the think-aloud process through teacher demonstration, the more skillful they become in making their own choices.

WHY IS CHOICE IMPORTANT?

"I liked making the board game. Can I make one for my next menu, too?"

—Second-grade student

One benefit of choice is its ability to meet the needs of so many different students and their learning styles. Teachers are aware that their students have different learning styles and understand the importance of accommodating different learning preferences in their classroom. In order to make this more feasible for teachers, the integration of choice can allow students to experience opportunities to find their niche. Unlike older elementary students, primary students have not been engaged in the learning process long enough to recognize their own strengths and weaknesses, as well as their preferred ways of learning; therefore, they need to be exposed to multiple options so they can begin to discover their preferences. By allowing choice, students are better able to narrow their options in the future and choose what best fits their learning preferences and educational needs.

Another benefit of choice is a greater sense of independence for the students. What a powerful feeling! This independence looks different at each grade level in the primary grades. It may be a kindergarten child working independently for an extended period time on a product he has selected or a second grader with special needs reading about a topic she has selected based on her interest. Once students understand that the goal is to produce *their* version of a task, that they will have the opportunity to design and create a product based on what they envision—they will really want to create something of their own. They will, however, still need some guidance and reassurance that their approach to a task is on the right track, so as teachers we are not out of a job by incorporating choice! The independence that structured choice at this level fosters simply allows us more time to facilitate and guide students in the direction they have selected for themselves. Allowing all of our students to show their learning by choosing the products they create helps develop independence at an early age at any ability level.

"I like getting to pick what I want."

—First-grade student

Strengthened student focus on the required content is a third benefit of choice. When students have choices in the activities they wish to complete, they are more focused on the learning that leads to their chosen product. Students become excited when they learn information that can help them develop a product they would like to create. Students will pay close attention to instruction and have an immediate application for the knowledge being presented in class. Also, if students are focused, they are less likely to be off task during instruction.

The final benefit (although I am sure there are many more) is the simple fact that by offering varied choices at appropriate levels, you can address implicit instructional options, explicit instructional options, and individual needs without anyone getting overly frustrated or overworked. There are few teaching strategies that can meet all of these different needs at once—it boils down to making the experience more personal for all of our students, and choice can do this.

Many a great educator has referred to the idea that the best learning takes place when students have a desire to learn and can feel successful while doing it. The majority of our primary students come to school with open minds, wanting to fill them with knowledge that is valuable and meaningful. By incorporating different activities from which to choose, students stretch beyond what they already know, and teachers create a void that needs to be filled. This void leads to a desire to learn.

HOW CAN PRIMARY TEACHERS PROVIDE CHOICES?

"I was pretty skeptical about using a menu with my [kids with special needs] since they need so many modifications, but I found that by using mainly graphics and cutting the menu like you suggested it was easy for them to grasp."

—First-grade teacher

When people go to a restaurant, the common goal is to find something on the menu to satisfy their hunger. Students come into our classrooms having a hunger as well—a hunger for learning. Choice menus are a way of allowing our students to choose how they would like to satisfy that hunger. At the very least, a menu is a list of choices that students use to choose an activity (or activities) they would like to complete to show what they have learned. At best, it is a complex system in which students earn points by making choices from different areas of study. Depending on the experience and comfort level of the students, the menus can also incorporate a free-choice option for those "picky eaters" who would like to place a special order to satisfy their learning hunger.

The next few sections provide examples of the types of menus that will be used in this book: target-based menus, in which students have a goal set by the design of the menu, and point-based menus, in which students select a product to reach a point goal. Each menu has its own benefits, limitations or drawbacks, and time considerations. An explanation of the free-choice option and its management will follow the information on each type of menu.

THREE-SHAPE MENU

"This was the easiest menu for me to modify for my students. Being able to cut it into pieces for those who needed less choice was a super easy modification!"

—Second-grade teacher

Description

The Three-Shape menu (see Figure 1) is a target-based menu with a total of nine predetermined choices for students. The choices are created at the various levels of Bloom's revised taxonomy (Anderson & Krathwohl, 2001) and incorporate different learning styles. All products carry the same weight for grading and have similar expectations for completion time and effort.

Benefits

Ease of modification. This menu can easily be modified by simply cutting the menu into strips of the same shape. As students complete a choice, they are given another strip of shapes. The choice

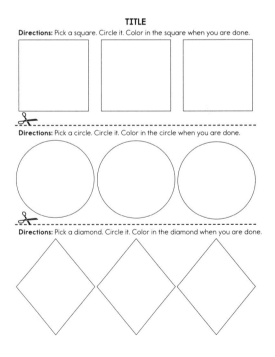

Figure 1. Three-Shape menu example.

then becomes one of three options, rather than three of nine, a much more daunting option.

Flexibility. This menu can cover either one topic in depth or three different objectives. When this menu covers just one objective, students have the option of completing three products: one from each shape group.

Friendly design. Students quickly understand how to use this menu. It is easy to explain how to make the choices based on the various shapes, and the shapes can be used to visually separate expectations (e.g., squares one day, circles the next).

Weighting. All products are equally weighted, so recording grades and maintaining paperwork are easily accomplished with this menu.

Short time period. This menu is intended for shorter periods of time, from one day to one week in the primary classroom.

Limitations

Few topics. This menu covers one or three topics.

Time Considerations

This menu usually is intended for shorter periods of completion time— at most, it should take one week in a primary inclusive classroom. If the menu focuses on one topic in depth, it can be completed in 1–2 days.

MEAL MENU

"Can I have dinner first?"

—Second-grade student with special needs in an inclusive classroom

Description

The Meal menu (see Figure 2) is a target-based menu with a total of at least nine predetermined choices as well as at least one enrichment option for students. The choices are created at the various levels of Bloom's revised taxonomy and incorporate different learning styles. All products carry the same weight for grading and have similar expectations for completion time and effort. The enrichment options can be used for extra credit or replace another meal option at the teacher's discretion.

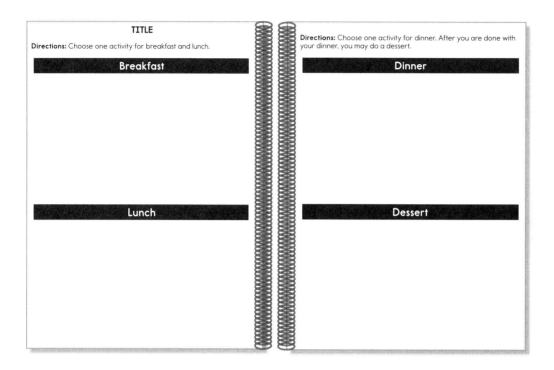

Figure 2. Meal menu example.

Benefits

Ease of modification. This menu can easily be modified by simply cutting the menu in half along its "spiral." Students first receive their breakfast and lunch choices; once completed, the teacher will provide the dinner and enriching dessert option. The choice can become one of six options, rather than 10 at once.

Flexibility. This menu can cover either one topic in depth or three different objectives. When this menu covers just one objective, students have the option of completing three products from different levels of Bloom's revised taxonomy: one for each meal.

Friendly design. Students quickly understand how to use this menu because of its real-world application.

Weighting. All products are equally weighted, so recording grades and maintaining paperwork are easily accomplished with this menu.

Short time period. This menu is intended for shorter periods of time, from one day to one week in the primary classroom.

Limitations

Few topics. This menu only covers one or three topics.

Time Considerations

This menu usually is intended for shorter periods of completion time—at most, it should take one week in a primary inclusive classroom. If the menu focuses on one topic in depth, it can be completed in 1–2 days.

TIC-TAC-TOE MENU

"At first, I thought it was a game, but it was really work—but then it was fun like a game."

—First-grade on-level student

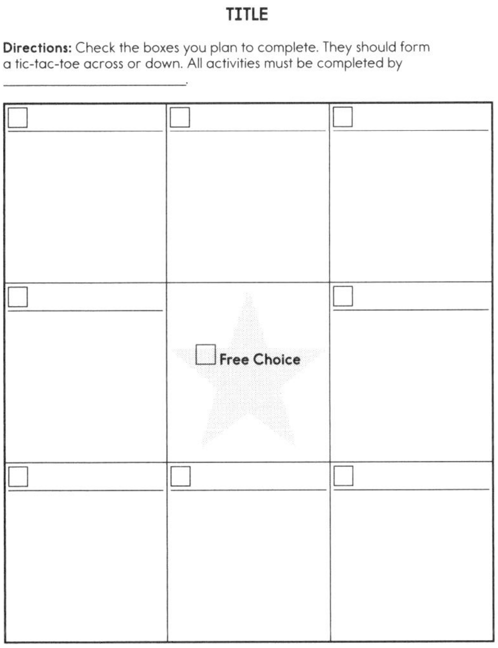

TITLE

Directions: Check the boxes you plan to complete. They should form a tic-tac-toe across or down. All activities must be completed by _____.

☐ Free Choice

Figure 3. Tic-Tac-Toe menu example.

Description

The Tic-Tac-Toe menu (see Figure 3) is a well-known, commonly used target-based menu that contains a total of eight predetermined choices and, if appropriate, one free choice for students. Choices can be created at the same level of Bloom's revised taxonomy or be arranged in a way to allow for three different levels or content areas. If all choices have been created at the same level of Bloom's revised taxonomy, each choice carries the same weight for grading and has similar expectations for completion time and effort.

Benefits

Flexibility. This menu can cover either one topic in depth or three different objectives. When this menu covers just one objective, all at the same level of Bloom's Revised taxonomy, students have the option of completing three products in a tic-tac-toe pattern or simply picking three from the menu.

When it covers three objectives or multiple levels of Bloom's revised taxonomy, students will need to complete a tic-tac-toe pattern (one in each column or row) to be sure they have completed one activity from each objective.

Challenge level. When students make choices on this menu to complete a row or column, based on its design, they will usually face one choice that is out of their comfort zone, be it for its level of Bloom's revised taxonomy, its product learning style, or its content. They will complete this "uncomfortable" choice because they want to do the other two options in that row or column.

Friendly design. Students quickly understand how to use this menu. It is nonthreatening because it does not contain points, therefore it seems to encourage students to stretch out of their comfort zones.

Weighting. All products are equally weighted, so recording grades and maintaining paperwork are easily accomplished with this menu.

Short time period. This menu is intended for shorter periods of time, between 1–3 weeks, although in a self-contained primary classroom, they can be completed within one week.

Limitations

Ease of modification. This menu does not lend itself to reducing the number of options that inclusive children often need when first approaching choice. It may not be as appropriate for a starter menu with these children.

Few topics. This menu only covers one or three topics.

Student compromise. Although this menu does allow for choice, a student will sometimes have to compromise and complete an activity he or she would not have chosen because it completes the required tic-tac-toe. (This is not always bad, though!)

Time Considerations

This menu usually is intended for shorter periods of completion time—at most, it should take 2–3 weeks in a primary inclusive classroom, with one product submitted each week. If the menu focuses on one topic in depth, it can be completed in one week.

PICK 3 MENU

"I started with the Pick 3 menu, although I just had my students pick any two—I wasn't too sure about jumping into three for their first menu. Most had no problem and wanted to do even more."

—First-grade teacher

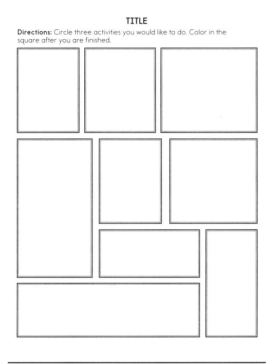

TITLE

Directions: Circle three activities you would like to do. Color in the square after you are finished.

Figure 4. Pick 3 menu example.

Description

The Pick 3 menu (see Figure 4) is a target-based menu that has a total of at least eight predetermined choices. These choices are placed randomly on the page, allowing students to select the target number as determined by the teachers. Choices are provided from different learning styles, as well as different levels of Bloom's revised taxonomy.

Benefits

Ease of modification. If the target number is three, the menu can be divided into three sections and the child selects one from each area. The target number can also easily be modified based on the ability of the child.

Weighting. All products are equally weighted, so recording grades and maintaining paperwork are easily accomplished with this menu.

Challenge level. When this menu is developed with multiple higher level activities, students will complete at least one activity at a higher level of Bloom's revised taxonomy in order to reach their target goal.

Intimidation level. The format of this menu is very student friendly, as it resembles other enjoyable activities often found at the primary grade levels.

Limitations

Few topics. This menu is best used for one topic in depth, although it can be used for up to three different topics, depending on its organization.

Cannot guarantee objectives. If the menu is used for more than one topic, it is possible for a student not to complete an activity for each objective, depending on the choices he or she makes.

Preparation. Teachers need to have all of the materials ready at the beginning of the unit for students to be able to choose any of the activities on the menu, which requires advanced planning.

Time Considerations

This menu usually is intended for shorter periods of completion time—at most, one week in a primary inclusive classroom.

TARGET-BASED LIST MENU

"I didn't think I would like it. It looked really hard but it was OK. I even got to use the computer to make something."

—Second-grade on-level student

Description

The Target-Based List menu (see Figure 5) has a total of at least 10 predetermined choices and at least one free choice for students. Choices are listed in such a way that all of the options are similar levels of Bloom's revised taxonomy, and the student is expected to complete a minimum number of activities.

Benefits

Ease of modification. Although the modification of this menu is not obvious, using a dark marker, teachers can divide the menu into smaller chunks. If the target number is three, the menu can be divided into three sections, and the child will select one from each area. The target number can also easily be modified based on the ability of the child.

Weighting. All products are equally weighted, so recording grades and maintaining paperwork are easily accomplished with this menu.

TITLE

Directions:
1. You may complete as many of the activities listed as you can within the time period.
2. You may choose any combination of activities. Your goal is to complete _____ activities.
3. You may be as creative as you like within the guidelines listed below.
4. You must share your plan with your teacher by _____.

Plan to Do	Activity to Complete	Completed
Total number of activities you are planning to complete:	Total number of activities completed:	

I am planning to complete _____ activities.

Teacher's initials _____ Student's signature _____

Figure 5. Target-Based List menu example.

Challenge level. When this menu is developed with multiple higher level activities, students will complete at least one activity at a higher level of Bloom's revised taxonomy in order to reach their target goal.

Limitations

Few topics. This menu is best used for one topic in depth, although it can be used for up to three different topics, depending on its organization.

Cannot guarantee objectives. If this menu is used for more than one topic, it is possible for a student not to have to complete an activity for each objective, depending on the choices he or she makes.

Preparation. Teachers need to have all of the materials ready at the beginning of the unit for students to be able to choose any of the activities on the list, which requires advanced planning.

Time Considerations

This menu usually is intended for shorter periods of completion time—at most, 2 weeks in a primary inclusive classroom.

GIVE ME 5 MENU

"I really liked the Give Me 5. I used it in February as my first 'real' menu. The students understood the goal of 5 and the choices were limited enough that it didn't overwhelm them—even my lowest [students] were successful."

—Kindergarten teacher

Description

A Give Me 5 point-based menu (see Figure 6) has activities worth two, three, or five points. It is a shorter variation on the 2-5-8 menu, with a total of at least six predetermined choices: at least two choices with a point value of two, at least two choices with a point value of three, and at least two choices with a point value of five. Choices are assigned these points based on the levels of Bloom's revised taxonomy. Choices with a point value of two represent the *remember* and *understand* levels; choices with a point value of three represent the *apply* and *analyze* levels; and choices with a point value of five represent the *evaluate* and *create* levels. Each level of choice carries different weights and has different expectations for completion time and effort. Students are expected to earn five points for a 100%, and they choose what combination they would like to use to attain that point goal. As with the 2-5-8 menu (see below), early primary teachers usually develop a way for students to understand their progress toward their point goals. Some will have students color the graphics along the bottom of the menu as they complete different point values, and some will give pennies, tokens, or tickets as each product is completed so students can see the concrete results of their efforts.

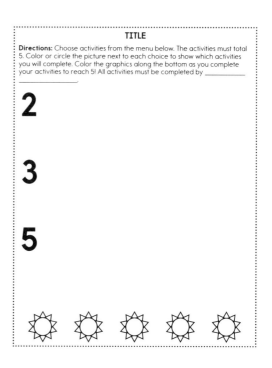

Figure 6. Give Me 5 menu example.

Benefits

Ease of modification. Being point-based, this menu allows the teacher and students to contract for different point values based on modifications, time constraints, and abilities. For example, rather than five points, a student with special needs could be given a goal of three as the target point value for 100%.

Responsibility. With this menu, students have complete control over their grades and/or how they reach their goals or target numbers. Although grades are not always a focus for students at the primary levels, it is a benefit for them to understand the basis of working toward a goal, be it a grade or a target number.

Appropriate challenge level. This menu's design is set up in such a way that students must complete at least one activity at a higher level of Bloom's revised taxonomy in order to reach their point goal; however, there is enough support to allow students with special needs to work their way up to the higher level with appropriate products.

Limitations

One topic. Although this menu can be used for more than one topic, it works best with in-depth study of one topic.

No free choice. By nature, it also does not allow students to propose their own free-choice activity, because point values need to be assigned based on Bloom's revised taxonomy.

Time Considerations

This menu usually is intended for shorter periods of completion time—at most, one week in a primary inclusive classroom; most self-contained teachers can complete this menu in 1–2 days.

2-5-8 MENU

"[The 2-5-8 menu] was fun. I got my 10 tickets and everything!"

—Kindergarten student

Description

A 2-5-8 menu (see Figure 7) is a point-based menu that is a longer version of the Give Me 5 menu; it has activities worth two, five, or eight points. It has a total of at least eight predetermined choices: at least two choices with a point value of two, at least four choices with a point value of five, and at least two choices with a point value of eight. Choices are assigned these point values based on the levels of Bloom's revised taxonomy. Choices with a point value of two represent the *remember* and *understand* levels; choices with a point value of five represent the *apply* and *analyze* levels; and choices with a point value of eight represent the *evaluate* and *create* levels. Each level of choice carries different weights and has different expectations for completion time and effort.

Students are expected to earn 10 points for a 100%, and they choose what combination they would like to use to attain that point goal. Early primary teachers usually develop a way for students to understand their progress toward their point goal. As with the Give Me 5 menu, some teachers will have students color the graphics along the bottom of the menu as they complete different point values, and some will give pennies, tokens, or tickets as each product is completed so students can see the concrete results of their efforts.

Benefits

Ease of modification. Being point-based, this menu allows the teacher and students to contract for different point values based on modifications, time constraints, and abilities. For example, rather than 10 points, a student with special needs could be given a goal of eight as the target point value for 100%.

Responsibility. With this menu, students have complete control over their grade and/or how they reach their goal or target number. Although grades are not always a focus for students at the primary levels, it is a benefit for them to understand the basis of working toward a goal, be it a grade or a target number.

Challenge level. This menu's design is set up in such a way that students must complete at least one activity at a higher level of Bloom's revised taxonomy in order to reach their point goal.

Limitations

One topic. Although this menu can be used for more than one topic, it works best with in-depth study of one topic.

No free choice. By nature, the menu does not automatically allow students to propose their own free choices, although it can be incorporated as a five- or eight-point option.

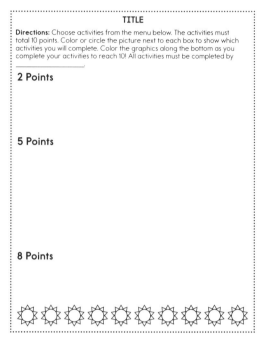

Figure 7. 2-5-8 menu example.

Limited challenge level. Students will complete only one activity at a higher level of thinking or, if contracted for other point values, could avoid the higher thinking options altogether.

Time Considerations

This menu usually is intended for shorter periods of completion time—at most, one week in a primary inclusive classroom.

POINT-BASED LIST MENU

"I like menus! I got to do a messy activity at the menu station cuz [sic] that is what I picked!"

—First-grade student interviewed about using menus in his classroom

Description

The Point-Based List menu (see Figure 8) has a total of at least eight predetermined choices, each with a designated point value, and at least one free choice for students. Choices are assigned points based on the levels of Bloom's revised taxonomy. The choices carry different weights and have different expectations for completion time and effort. A point criterion is established that equals 100%, and students choose how they wish to attain that point goal.

Benefits

Ease of modification. Being point-based, this menu allows the teacher and students to contract for different point values based on modifications, time constraints, and abilities. For example, rather

TITLE

Directions:
1. You may complete as many of the activities listed as you can within the time period.
2. You may choose any combination of activities. Your goal is 20 points.
3. You must share your plan with your teacher by _____.
4. Activities may be turned in at any time during the working time period. They will be graded and recorded on this sheet as you continue to work, so keep it safe!

Plan to Do	Activity to Complete	Point Value	Completed	Points Earned
	Total number of activities you are planning to complete:	Total number of activities completed:		

I am planning to complete _____ activities, which could earn up to a total of _____ points.

Teacher's initials _____ Student's signature _____

Figure 8. Point-Based List menu example.

than 20 points, a student could be contracted for 15 as the target point value for a 100%.

Responsibility. Students have complete control over their grades. Students like the idea that they can guarantee their grade if they complete the required work. If they lose points on one of the chosen assignments, they can complete another activity to be sure they have met their point goal.

Concept reinforcement. This menu also allows for an in-depth study of material; however, if the menu uses the different levels of Bloom's revised taxonomy, students who are still learning the concepts can choose some of the lower level point value projects to reinforce the basics before jumping into the higher level activities.

Limitations

For choice-ready students. This menu has a lot of choices for primary students. They have to be comfortable with this amount of choice, working with larger numbers, and understanding their grades. Some primary students are ready for this level of choice; others will not be ready until upper elementary.

Few topics. This menu is best used for one topic in depth, although it can be used for up to three different topics, depending on its organization.

Cannot guarantee objectives. If this menu is used for more than one topic, it is possible for a student not to have to complete an activity for each objective, depending on the choices he or she makes.

Preparation. Teachers need to have all of the materials ready at the beginning of the unit for students to be able to choose any of the activities on the list, which requires advanced planning.

Time Considerations

This menu usually is intended for shorter periods of completion time—at most, 2 weeks in a primary inclusive classroom.

FREE CHOICE IN THE INCLUSIVE PRIMARY CLASSROOM

"I decided to not include free choice on my menus until right before the end of the year. [The students] just weren't ready. I had a few do some neat projects though when I did."

—First-grade teacher

Many of the menus included in this book allow students to submit a free-choice product. This is a product of their choosing that addresses the content being studied and shows what the student has learned about the topic. Although this option is available, students may not fully understand its benefits or immediately respond to the opportunity even after it has been explained. In the past, certain students may have been offered choices and enjoyed the idea of taking charge of their own learning, however, students with special needs may not have had much exposure to this concept. Their educational experiences tend to be objective based and teacher-driven. This is not to say that they would not respond well to the idea of free choice; in fact, they can embrace it enthusiastically. Students with special needs need to feel confident in their knowledge of the content and information before they are ready to step out on their own, propose their own ideas, and create their own products.

Figure 9 shows two sample proposal forms that have been used successfully with primary students when the students are allowed to submit a free choice for their teacher's consideration. If the teacher has decided that his or her students have had enough exposure to different products and are ready to work independently, a copy of these forms can be given to each student when a menu that includes a free choice option is first introduced. The form used is based on the type of menu being presented. For example, if you are using the Tic-Tac-Toe or Meal menu, there is no need to submit a point proposal.

A discussion should be held with the students so they understand the expectations of a free choice. There are always a few students who do not want to complete a task on the menu or have their own idea of what they would like to do; they are welcome to create their own free choice product and submit it for approval. The more free choice is used and encouraged, the more students will begin to request it. How the students show their

Name: _____ Teacher's Approval: _____

FREE-CHOICE PROPOSAL FORM

Proposal Outline

1. What will you learn about? _____

_____

_____

2. What will it look like?_____

_____

_____

3. What will you need from the teacher to make it? _____

_____

Name: _____ Teacher's Approval: _____

FREE-CHOICE PROPOSAL FORM
FOR POINT-BASED MENU

I want to create something for _____ points. Points Approval: _____

Proposal Outline

1. What will you learn about? _____

_____

2. What will it look like?_____

_____

_____

3. What will you need from the teacher to make it? _____

_____

Figure 9. Sample proposal forms for free choice.

knowledge will begin to shift from teacher-focused to student-designed activities. If students do not want to make a proposal using the proposal form after the teacher has discussed the entire menu and its activities, they can place the unused form in a designated place in the classroom. Others may want to use the form, and it is often surprising who wants to submit a proposal form after hearing about the opportunity.

Proposal forms must be submitted before students begin working on their free-choice products. The teacher then knows what the students are working on, and the students know the expectations the teacher has for their products. Once approved, the forms can be stapled to the students' menu sheets. The students can refer to their own form as they develop their free-choice product, and when the grading takes place, the teacher can refer to the agreement for the graded features of the product.

As a note, although all of the above considerations rely on the students to complete their own proposal form, this should not deter students whose writing skills are not at the same level as their verbal skills. Although it would be wonderful if all of the children could complete and submit their own proposal forms, that is not always the case. In fact, those students who have strong verbal and artistic skills may want to create a product that showcases their ability but the proposal form itself hinders them. After discussing the option of free choice, it is always recommended that the teacher offer to help students fill out their free-choice form if there is something else that they would really like to create. When children who are struggling are temporarily freed from a written task, it is amazing what they can create to show their learning.

Each part of the proposal form is important and needs to be discussed with students.

- *Name/Teacher's Approval.* The student or teacher will fill in the student's name. The student must submit this form to the teacher for approval. The teacher will carefully review all of the information, discuss any suggestions or alterations with the student, if needed, and then sign the top.
- *Points Requested.* Found only on the point-based menu proposal form, this is where negotiation may need to take place. Students usually will submit their first request for a very high number (even the 100% goal). They tend to equate the amount of time something will take with the number of points it should earn. But please note that the points are always based on the levels of Bloom's revised

taxonomy and its appropriate alignment with the student's age and ability level. For example, students may be asked to apply what they know to a new situation, perhaps by making a set of concentration cards about animals they have not studied. This would be a higher level activity for a kindergarten student, but a middle-level activity for a second grader because Bloom's revised taxonomy is developmental in nature.

- *Points Approved.* Found only on the point-based menu proposal form, this is the final decision recorded by the teacher once the point haggling is finished.
- *Proposal Outline.* This is where the student will describe the product he or she intends to complete. Primary students may need some assistance refining and narrowing their ideas. Teachers should ask questions to understand what students plan to complete, as well as to ensure student understanding. This also shows the teacher that the student knows what he or she is planning on completing.
  o *What will you learn about?* Students need to be specific here. It is not acceptable to write *science* or *reading*. This is where they look at the objectives of the product and choose which objective their product demonstrates.
  o *What will it look like?* It is important for this section to be as detailed as possible. If a student cannot express what the product will look like, he or she probably has not given the free-choice plan enough thought.
  o *What will you need from the teacher to make it?* This is an important consideration. Sometimes students do not have the means to purchase items for their product. This can be negotiated, but if teachers ask students to think about what they may need, they will often develop even grander ideas for their free choice product.

CHAPTER 2

How to Use Menus in the Inclusive Primary Classroom

There are different ways to use instructional product-based menus in the inclusive classroom. In order to decide how to implement each menu, the following questions should be considered: How much prior knowledge of the topic being taught do the students have before the unit or lesson begins, how confident are your students in making choices and working independently, and how much intellectually and/or developmentally appropriate information is readily available for students to obtain on their own? After considering these questions, there are a variety of ways to use menus in the classroom.

RECALLING OR BUILDING BACKGROUND KNOWLEDGE

There are many ways to use menus in the classroom. One way that is often overlooked is using menus to review or build background knowledge before a unit begins. This is frequently used when first- and second-grade students have had exposure to upcoming content in the past, perhaps during the previous year's instruction or through similar life experiences. Although they may have been exposed to the content previously, students may not remember the details of the content at the level needed to proceed with this year's unit immediately. A shorter menu covering the previous year's objectives can be provided in the day or week prior to the new unit so that students have the opportunity to recall and engage with the information in a meaningful way. They will then be ready to take their knowledge to a deeper level during the unit. For example, a few days before starting a unit on addition, the teacher may select a short menu on representing numbers using manipulatives, knowing that the students have had the content in the past and should be able to successfully work independently on the menu by engaging their prior knowledge. Students work on basic products from the menu as anchor activities throughout the week preceding the addition unit, with all products being submitted prior to the unit's initiation. This way, the students have been in a "number frame of mind" independently for a week and are ready to investigate the topic further.

ENRICHMENT AND SUPPLEMENTAL ACTIVITIES

Using the menus for enrichment and supplemental activities is the most common way of using menus. In this case, the students usually do not have a lot of background knowledge, and information about the topic may not be readily available to all students. The teacher will introduce the menu and the activities at the beginning of a unit. The teacher then will progress through the content at the normal rate using his or her curricular materials, periodically allowing class and perhaps center time throughout the unit for students to work on their menu choices to supplement the lessons being taught. This method is very effective, as it incorporates an immediate use for the content the teacher is covering. For example, at the beginning of a unit on subtraction, the teacher may introduce the menu with the explanation that students may not yet have enough knowledge to complete all of their choices. During the unit, however, more content will be provided and the students will be prepared to work on new choices. If students want to work ahead, they can certainly find the information on their own, but that is not required. Although some students often see this as a challenge and will begin to investigate concepts mentioned in the menu before the teacher has discussed them, other students begin to develop questions about the concepts and are ready to ask them when the teacher covers the material. This helps build an immense pool of background knowledge and possible content questions before the topic is even discussed in the classroom. This way, primary students are more likely to be excited about the topic and are ready to discuss and question the new content as it is presented. By introducing a menu at the beginning of a unit and allowing students to complete products as instruction progresses, we encourage the students to naturally investigate the information and come to class prepared.

COMPACTING

Within any primary classroom, there are diverse knowledge and ability levels that can vary based on the content being studied or even the topic within a content. Compacting, or preassessing students and then offering alternatives for any student who shows mastery, is often used to address these diverse abilities. Given the task of compacting curricular units, teachers are often frustrated by locating alternative options to replace certain activities and lessons for those students who have "tested out." A common solution is setting up a preassessment with the stipulation that only if a student tests out of a unit completely will an alternate assignment be available, thereby decreasing the number of alternative options a teacher would need to find or create. This solution, although practical, may guarantee that students with special needs never have the opportunity to compact their learning, even for a unit for which they may have a lot of knowledge. The best model of compacting allows students, no matter their ability level, who show proficiency in just one piece or aspect of the unit of study to complete an alternate assignment. Menus can be used to serve this purpose. Whether students test out of an entire unit that is their passion area or show proficiency in just one aspect, activities can be selected and offered to replace the standard instruction. If the entire class has access to the menu for enrichment, students whose curricula have been compacted may be contracted to choose between certain options to be completed, thereby replacing the planned curricular activities that they have already mastered.

STANDARD ACTIVITIES

Another option for using menus in the classroom is to replace certain curricular activities the teacher uses to teach the specified content. In this case, the students may have some limited background knowledge about the content, and appropriately leveled information is readily available for them in their classroom resources. The teacher would pick and choose which aspects of the content must be directly taught to the students and which could be appropriately learned and reinforced through product menus. The unit would then be designed using a mixture of formal large-group lessons, small-group lessons, and specific menu times (often through centers) where the students would use the menu to reinforce their prior knowledge. In order for this option to be effective, the teacher must feel very comfortable with the students' prior knowledge level. Although there are a few occasions when menus could be used this way with kindergarten students, this is more for second-semester first and second graders.

Another variation on this method that is appropriate for kindergarten students is using the menus to drive center activities. Centers have many different functions in the classroom—most importantly, reinforcing the instruction that has taken place. Rather than having a set rotation for centers, the teacher could use the menu activities as enrichment or supplemental activities during center time for those students who need more than just reinforcement; centers could be set up with any materials students would need to complete their products.

CHAPTER 3

Product Guidelines

"I just don't know what I want to do. Maybe something with markers."

—Kindergarten student

This chapter outlines the different types of products included in the featured menus, as well as the guidelines and expectations for each. It is very important that students know the expectations of a completed product when they choose to work on it. By discussing and demonstrating these expectations *before* students begin, and by having information readily available for students, the teacher can limit frustration on everyone's part.

It is very important to note that when using the product guidelines—or products in general—with primary inclusive students, the students need to have some experience with the product in a whole-class setting before being asked to create their own. This means that the teacher may need to spend some time during the first weeks of school integrating the types of products into lessons that the students will encounter in their menus later on in the year. The guidelines will then simply serve as a visual clue to remind the children about the product outlined in the task.

$1 CONTRACT

I did not spend more than $1.00 on my _____

_____   _____

Student Signature   Date

My child, _____, did not spend more than $1.00 on the product he or she created.

_____   _____

Parent Signature   Date

Figure 10. $1 contract example.

$1 CONTRACT

Consideration should be given to the cost of creating the products featured on any menu. The resources available to students vary within a classroom, and students should not be graded on the amount of materials they can purchase to make their products look better. These menus are designed to equalize the resources students have available. The materials for most products are available for less than a dollar and can usually be found in a teacher's classroom as part of the classroom supplies. If a product requires materials from the student, there is a $1 contract as part of the product criteria. This is a very important part of the explanation of the product. First of all, limiting the amount of money a child (or his or her parents) can spend creates an equal amount of resources for all students. Second, it actually encourages a more creative product. When students are limited by the amount of materials they can readily purchase, they often have to use materials from home in new and unique ways. Figure 10 shows a sample $1 contract that has been used many times in my classroom for various products.

THE PRODUCTS

Table 1 contains a list of the products used in this book and additional products that can be used as free-choice ideas. These products were chosen for their flexibility in meeting learning styles, for their appropriateness for primary students, and for being products many teachers already encourage in their classrooms. They have been arranged by learning style—visual, kinesthetic, and auditory—and each menu has been designed to include products appropriate for all learning styles. Some of the best products cross over between different categories; however, they have been listed here by how they are presented or implemented in the menus.

Product Frustrations

One of the biggest frustrations that accompany the use of these various products on the menus is the barrage of questions about the products themselves. Students can become so wrapped up in the products and the criteria for creating them that they do not focus on the content being presented. This is especially true when menus are first introduced to the class. Students can spend an exorbitant amount of time asking the teacher about the products mentioned on a menu. When this happens, what should have been a 10–15-minute menu introduction turns into 45–50 minutes of discussion about product expectations. In order to facilitate the introduction of the menu products, teachers should have on hand examples of the products students have already created with guidance from the teacher. This, in addition to the product guideline, is usually enough to trigger their memory about a specific product.

Teachers may consider showing students examples of the product(s) from the previous year. Although this can be helpful, it can also lead to additional frustration on the part of both the teacher and the students. Some students may not feel that they can produce a product as nice, as big, as special, or as (you fill in the blank) as the example, or when shown an example, students might interpret that as meaning that the teacher would like something exactly like the one he or she showed to students. To avoid this situation, I would propose that when using examples, the example students are shown be a "blank" one that demonstrates how to create only the shell of the product. If an example of a windowpane is needed, for instance, students might be shown a blank piece of paper that is divided into six panes. The students can then take the skeleton of the product and

Table 1
PRODUCTS

Visual	Kinesthetic	Auditory
Acrostic	Board Game	Children's Book
Advertisement	Bulletin Board Display	Commercial
Book Cover	Class Game	Demonstration
Brochure/Pamphlet	Collection	News Report
Bulletin Board Display	Commercial	Play/Skit
Cartoon/Comic Strip	Concentration Cards	PowerPoint–Presentation
Children's Book	Cube	Presentation of Created Product
Collage	Demonstration	Puppet
Crossword Puzzle	Diorama	Song/Rap
Diary/Journal	Flipbook	Speech
Drawing	Folded Quiz Book	Tell a Story
Essay/Research Report	Jigsaw Puzzle	You Be the Person Presentation
Folded Quiz Book	Mobile	
Greeting Card	Model	
Instruction Card	Mural	
Letter	Mystery Object	
List	Play/Skit	
Map	Puppet	
Mind Map	Show and Tell	
Newspaper Article		
Paragraph		
Picture Dictionary		
Poster		
PowerPoint–Stand Alone		
Scrapbook		
Story–Written		
Trading Cards		
Venn Diagram		
Windowpane		

make it their own as they create their own version of the windowpane using their information.

Product Guidelines

Most frustrations associated with products can be addressed proactively through the introduction of the product in a whole-class setting and the use of standardized, predetermined product guidelines that are shared with students prior to them creating any products. These product guidelines are designed in a specific yet generic way, such that any time throughout the school year that the students select a product, that product's guidelines will apply. A beneficial side effect of using set guidelines for a product is the security it creates. Students are often reticent to try something new, as doing so requires taking a risk. Traditionally, when students select a product, they ask questions about creating it, hope they remember and understood all of the details, and turn it in. It can be quite a surprise when they receive the product back and realize that it was not complete or was not what was expected. As you can imagine, students may not want to take a risk on something new the next time; they often prefer to do what they know and be successful. Through the use of product guidelines, students can begin to feel secure in their choice before they start working on a new product. If they are not feeling secure, they tend to stay within their comfort zone.

The product guidelines for menu products included in this book, as well as some potential free-choice options, are included in an easy-to-read card format that was selected especially for inclusive students (see Figure 11) with a graphic that depicts the guidelines for each product. (The guidelines for some products, such as presentation of created product, are omitted because teachers often have their own criteria for these products.) These guideline cards are convenient for students to have in front of them when they work on their products. Each card has a graphic that should trigger their recall of the product they have previously created with their teacher as well as illustrate most of the important criteria stated on the product card. These graphics are also found on each menu. They are the focal point of the lower level menus ▲, which have fewer words, and the graphics are next to the task statements that require the corresponding product on the on-level menus ●. This allows students to easily match a product with its criteria if teachers are using the product guidelines.

There really is no one right way to share the product guideline information with your students. It all depends on their abilities and needs. Some second-grade teachers choose to duplicate and distribute all of the product guidelines pages to students at the beginning of the year so each child has his or her own copy while working on products. As another option, a few classroom sets can be created by gluing each product guideline card onto a separate index card, hole punching the corner of each card, and placing all of the cards on a metal ring. These ring sets can be placed in a central location or at centers where students can borrow and return them as they work on their products. This allows for the addition of products as they are introduced. Some teachers prefer to introduce the product guidelines and their specific graphics as students experience products through whole-class activities. In this case, the product guidelines may be enlarged, laminated, and posted on a bulletin board for easy access and reference during classroom work. Some teachers prefer to give only a few product guidelines at a time, while others may feel it is appropriate to provide more cards when students start feeling comfortable enough to develop their own free choice product. The cards for the products mentioned in a specific menu can also be reduced in size and copied onto the back of that menu so they are available when students want to refer to them. Students enjoy looking at all of the different product options, and they may get new ideas as they peruse the guidelines. No matter which method teachers choose to share the information with the students, they will save themselves a lot of time and frustration by having the product guidelines available for student reference (e.g., "Look at your product guidelines—I think that will answer your question").

ACROSTIC

Write the word
Oval letters
Remember the word
Draw a picture

- White piece of paper
- Written neatly
- Main word on the left-hand side
- 1 phrase for each letter
- Phrases must be about the main word

ADVERTISEMENT

Information

$8.00

Nice, White Shirt

- White piece of paper
- Draw and color the picture of item or service
- Include price, if needed

BOARD GAME

- At least 4 game pieces
- At least 20 colored squares
- At least 10 question cards
- Title of the game on the game board
- Explain rules of the game
- At least the size of a file folder

BOOK COVER

- Front cover—include title, author, and picture
- Cover inside flap—write a paragraph or sentences about the book
- Back inside flap—provide information about the author with at least 3 facts
- Back cover—tell whether you liked the book and why
- Spine—include title and author

Figure 11. Product guidelines.

BROCHURE/PAMPHLET

- White piece of paper
- Fold the paper
- Title and picture on the front page
- At least 5 facts inside

BULLETIN BOARD DISPLAY

- Has to fit on a bulletin board or wall
- At least 5 facts
- Has a title
- Needs to be creative

CARTOON/COMIC STRIP

- White piece of paper
- At least 6 squares or cells
- Have characters talk to each other
- Use color

CHILDREN'S BOOK

- Cover with the title and your name
- At least 10 pages
- Picture on each page
- Written neatly

Figure 11. Continued.

CLASS GAME

- Needs easy rules
- Include questions for your classmates
- Can be like a game you know how to play

COLLAGE

- White piece of paper
- Cut pictures neatly
- Use magazines or newspapers
- Glue pictures neatly on the paper
- Label pictures

COLLECTION

- Has the number of items needed
- Fit items inside area
- Bring in a box or bag
- No living things

COMMERCIAL

- 1–2 minutes in length
- Presented to classmates or recorded ahead of time
- Use props or costumes
- Can have more than 1 person in it

Figure 11. Continued.

CONCENTRATION CARDS

- At least 20 cards (10 matching sets)
- Has pictures, words, or both
- Write on only 1 side of each card
- Include an answer key that shows the matches
- In a bag or envelope

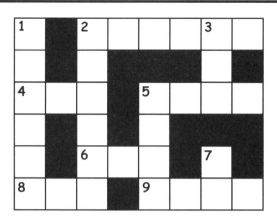

CROSSWORD PUZZLE

- At least 15 words
- Provide clues for each word
- Include puzzle and answer key
- Can be made on the computer

CUBE

- Use all 6 sides of the cube to provide information
- Written neatly or made on the computer
- Print your name neatly on the bottom of 1 of the sides
- Should be turned in flat (unfolded) for grading

DEMONSTRATION

- At least 1 minute
- Show all important information
- Include 2 questions for classmates
- Be able to answer questions from classmates

Figure 11. Continued.

DIARY/JOURNAL

- Written neatly or made on the computer
- Write at least 1 page for each day
- Has the date on each page
- Write as if you are the character

DIORAMA

- Use a box
- Glue pictures and information on the inside walls of box
- Write your name on the back
- Write information about the diorama on a card
- Fill out a $1 contract

DRAWING

- White piece of paper
- Use colors
- Drawn neatly
- Has a title
- Write your name on the back

ESSAY/RESEARCH REPORT

- Written neatly or made on the computer
- Includes enough information about the topic
- Write the information in your own words (no copying from books or the Internet!)

Figure 11. Continued.

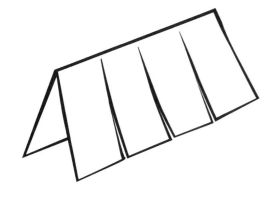

FLIPBOOK

- White piece of paper folded in half
- Cut flaps into the top
- Use color for the drawings
- Write your name on the back

FOLDED QUIZ BOOK

- Folded white paper
- At least 8 questions
- Write the questions on the outside flaps
- Write the answers inside each flap
- Write your name on the back

GREETING CARD

- Front—include colored pictures (words are optional)
- Front inside—include a personal note
- Back inside—include a greeting, saying, or poem
- Back outside—include your name and price of card

INSTRUCTION CARD

- Use large blank or lined index card
- Written neatly or made on the computer
- Use color for drawings
- Provide clear instructions

Figure 11. Continued.

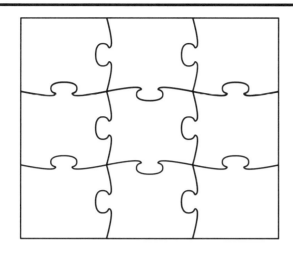

JIGSAW PUZZLE

- Use cardstock
- At least 9 pieces
- Use color
- May have words
- Makes a picture when finished

LETTER

- Written neatly or made on the computer
- Follow letter format
- Include all needed information

LIST

- Written neatly or made on the computer
- Include the number of items required
- Very complete
- Include words or phrases for each letter of alphabet except X for alphabet lists

MAP

- White piece of paper
- Information is correct and accurate
- At least 8 locations
- Include a compass rose, legend, scale, and key

Figure 11. Continued.

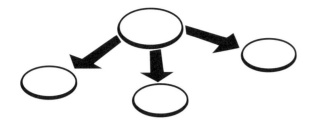

MIND MAP

- White piece of unlined paper
- 1 word in the middle
- No more than 4 words coming from any 1 word
- Written neatly or made on the computer

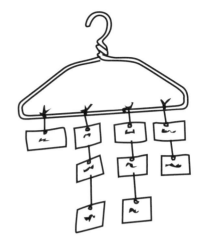

MOBILE

- At least 10 pieces of information
- Include color and pictures
- Include at least 3 layers of hanging information
- Hangs straight

MODEL

- At least 8" × 8" × 12"
- Label the parts of the model
- Include a title card
- Use recycled materials
- Write your name on the model

MURAL

- Size of a poster board or bigger
- At least 5 pieces of information
- Color the pictures on the mural
- May include words; must include a title
- Write your name on the back

Figure 11. Continued.

MYSTERY OBJECT

- Put your object in a box
- At least 4 clues so others can guess
- No living things

NEWS REPORT

- Tell who, what, where, when, why, and how the event happened
- Can be presented to classmates or recorded ahead of time

NEWSPAPER ARTICLE

- Should describe what happened
- Design it to look like a newspaper article
- Include a picture to go with article
- Include all relevant information
- Written neatly or made on the computer

> The sky is blue today. I see a boat on the lake and a man fishing. There is a bird singing in the tree outside my window. I will soon eat breakfast and go for a bike ride with my friend Julie. It is a good day.

PARAGRAPH

- Written neatly or made on the computer
- Must have topic sentence, at least 3 supporting sentences or details, and a concluding sentence
- Must use vocabulary and punctuation

Figure 11. Continued.

PICTURE DICTIONARY

- Written neatly or made on the computer
- Have a clear picture for each word
- Draw pictures
- Use your own words for definitions

PLAY/SKIT

- 3–5 minutes in length
- Turn in written script before play is presented
- Present to classmates or record ahead of time
- Use props or costumes
- Can have more than 1 person in it

POSTER

- Use poster board
- At least 5 pieces of important information
- Must have a title
- Use both words and pictures
- Write your name on the back
- Include a bibliography as needed

POWERPOINT— PRESENTATION

- At least 8 slides, plus a title slide with your name
- Use color in slides
- No more than 1 picture per page
- Can use animation, but limit it
- Should be timed to flow with the oral presentation

Figure 11. Continued.

POWERPOINT— STAND ALONE

- At least 8 slides, plus a title slide with your name
- Use color in slides
- No more than 10 words on each page
- No more than 1 picture per page
- Can use animation, but limit how much

PUPPET

- Should be handmade and have a moveable mouth
- List supplies used to make the puppet
- Use recycled materials
- Sign a $1 contract
- If used in a play, all play criteria must be met as well

SCRAPBOOK

- Include a meaningful title and your name on the cover
- At least 4 pages in length
- At least 1 picture on each page
- Captions for all pictures

SHOW AND TELL

- Bring 1 thing to school
- Tell 3 things about it
- Answer at least 1 question

Figure 11. Continued.

SONG/RAP

- At least 1 minute in length
- Should be able to understand all words in the song/rap
- Can be a familiar tune
- Can be presented to classmates or recorded ahead of time
- Turn in written words

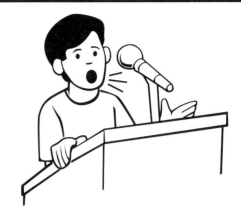

SPEECH

- At least 1 minute in length
- Speak clearly and loudly
- Try not to read directly from your paper
- Turn in the written speech before you speak

STORY—WRITTEN

- Include all of the elements of a well-written story
- Should be long enough for the story to make sense
- Written neatly or made on the computer

TELL A STORY

- Include all of the elements of a well-written story
- Should be long enough for the story to make sense
- Told to teacher or recorded on a computer

Figure 11. Continued.

TRADING CARDS

- At least 8 cards
- At least 3" × 5"
- Colored picture on each card
- At least 3 facts on each card
- Can have information on both sides
- Turn in cards in a carrying bag

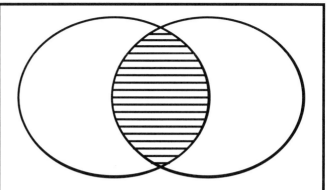

VENN DIAGRAM

- A piece of paper turned lengthwise
- Include a title at the top
- Include a title for each circle
- At least 6 items in each part

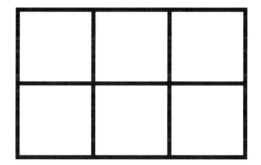

WINDOWPANE

- White piece of paper
- At least 6 squares
- Include a picture and words in each square
- Written neatly or made on the computer
- Be creative
- Write your name on the back

YOU BE THE PERSON PRESENTATION

- Pretend to be the person
- 1–3 minutes in length
- At least 5 facts about his or her life
- Present to classmates
- Be able to answer questions about your character
- Use props or a costume

Figure 11. Continued.

CHAPTER 4

Rubrics and Graphing Grading

"I think rubrics are important, although we do not really focus on number grades first semester. I think they do share my expectations and it is not a bad thing for the students to understand the concept of expectations."

—First-grade teacher, when asked about the importance of rubrics

The most common reason teachers feel uncomfortable with menus is the need for equal grading. Teachers often feel that it is easier to grade the same type of product made by all of the students than to grade a large number of different products, none of which looks like any other. The great equalizer for hundreds of different products is a generic rubric that can cover all of the important qualities of an excellent product.

ALL-PURPOSE RUBRIC

When it comes to primary students and rubrics, it is often difficult to find a format that is effective in enhancing students' products. The purpose of a rubric is to demonstrate for the students the criteria and expectations of the teacher, as well as to allow the teacher to quickly evaluate a product using these same criteria. When designing a rubric for primary students, it is important to look at what would be meaningful to them. It should also be noted that many kindergarten and first-grade programs do not give formal grades for student work. This should be taken into account when using a rubric.

Figure 12 is an example of a rubric that has been classroom tested in the primary grades with students of various ability levels to encourage quality products. When number grades are assigned, this rubric can be used with any point value activity presented in a point-based menu. When a menu is presented to students, this rubric can be reproduced on the back of the menu with its guidelines or shared with the students along with examples. The first time students see this rubric, it can be explained in detail using the graphics as a guide. This rubric was designed to be specific enough to allow students to understand the criteria the teacher is seeking, but general enough that they can still be as creative as they like in the creation of their products.

Name:_____

ALL-PURPOSE PRODUCT RUBRIC

	Excellent	Good	Poor
Completeness Is everything included in the product?	All information needed is included.	Some important information is missing.	Most important information is missing.
Creativity Is the product original?	Information is creative. Graphics are original.	Information is creative. Graphics are not original or were found on the computer.	There is no evidence of new thoughts or perspectives in the product.
Correctness Is all of the information included correct?	All information in the product is correct and accurate.		Any portion of the information presented is incorrect.
Appropriate Communication Is the information well communicated?	All information is neat, easy to read, and easy to understand if presented.	Most of the product is neat, easy to read, and loud enough if presented.	The product is not neat or it is not easy to read.
Effort and Time Did student put significant effort into the product?	Effort is obvious.		The product does not show significant effort.

Figure 12. All-purpose rubric.

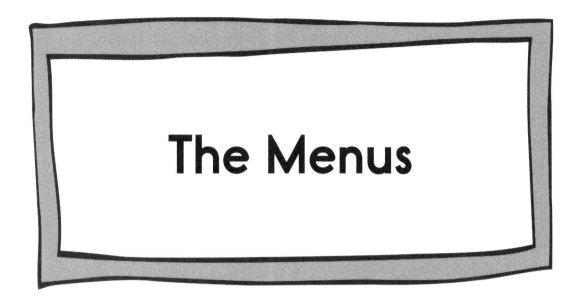

The Menus

HOW TO USE THE MENU PAGES

Each topic in this section has:
- an introduction page for the teacher;
- a lower level content menu, indicated by a triangle ▲ in the upper right-hand corner;
- an on-level content menu, indicated by a circle ● in the upper right-hand corner
- any specific guidelines for the menu, and
- activities mentioned in the menu.

The lower level menus ▲, which are appropriate for lower level readers, include large graphics of the products with fewer words (typically short phrases) to keep the students' focus on the graphics. If a teacher is unsure about a shortened task, a quick glance at the on-level menu ● for that same topic should clarify any questions, as these menus use both graphics and complete sentences to express each task.

INTRODUCTION PAGES

The introduction pages for each topic are meant to provide an overview of each set of menus. They are divided into the following areas:

- *Title and Menu Type*: The top of each introductory page will tell you the main topic covered by the menus as well as the menu type(s) used. Each topic included has two menus, one for lower level students ▲ and one for on-level students ●. In order to modify for students with special needs, the lower level menu focuses more on graphics and may have a different format to control the amount of choice a student faces at one time.

- *Objectives Covered Through These Menus and Activities*. This area will list all of the objectives that the menus address. Menus are arranged in such a way that if students complete the guidelines set forth in the instructions, all of these objectives will be covered. Some objectives may be designated with a ▲ or a ●, which indicates that a particular objective is only addressed on its corresponding menu.

- *Materials Needed by Students for Completion*. For each menu, it is expected that the teacher will provide, or students will have access to, the following materials:
  - lined paper;
  - glue;
  - crayons, colored pencils, or markers; and
  - blank 8.5" × 11" white paper.

  The introduction page also includes a list of additional materials that may be needed by students. Because students have the choice of which menu items they would like to complete, it is possible that the teacher will not need all of the additional materials for every student.

- *Special Notes on the Modifications of These Menus*. Some menu formats have special management issues or considerations when it comes to modifying for different ability levels. This section will review additional options available for modifying a menu.

- *Special Notes on the Use of These Menus*. This section will share any tips to consider for a specific menu format, activity, or product.

- *Time Frame.* Each menu has its own ideal time frame based on its structure, but all menus work best given at least one day or up to a week time frame. Menus that assess more objectives are better suited to time frames of up to 2 weeks. This section will give you an overview about the best time frame for completing the menus, as well as options for shorter time periods. If teachers do not have time to devote to an entire menu, they can certainly choose the one-day option for any topic students are currently studying.
- *Suggested Forms.* This section lists the rubrics that should be available for students as the menus are introduced. If a menu has a free-choice option, the appropriate proposal form will also be listed here.

CHAPTER 5

Numbers and Number Sense Menus

NUMBER WORDS

MEAL MENU

Objectives Covered Through This Menu and These Activities

- Students will connect number words, numbers, and graphical representations.
- Students will correctly use number words in different situations.

Materials Needed by Students for Completion

- Poster board or large white paper
- Blank index cards (for concentration cards and trading cards)
- Large blank or lined index cards (for instruction cards)
- Graph paper or Internet access (for crossword puzzle) ●
- Number Words Jigsaw Puzzle template ▲
- Magazines (for collages)
- Materials for board games (folders, colored cards, etc.)

Special Notes on the Modifications of These Menus

- The Meal menu format has a design feature that makes it easy to reduce the number of choices students face at one time. Students can be given the left side (breakfast and lunch, or lower levels of thinking) as their first options. After these two meal products have been completed, students can then receive the right side (dinner and dessert, or higher levels of thinking and enrichment options). After becoming accustomed to the amount of choice, students can then get the entire meal menu at once.

Special Notes on the Use of These Menus

- The lower level menu ▲ is specifically designed for students who are lower level readers or for those with a more limited vocabulary. It is meant to simply remind students of product options that have already been explained.

Time Frame

- 1 week—Students are given a menu as the unit is started. As the unit progresses throughout the week, students should refer back to the menu options associated with that content. The teacher will go over all of the options for that content and have students color or circle the graphic for each option that represents the activity they are most interested in completing. As teaching continues, the activities chosen and completed should create a full day's meal, with a breakfast, a lunch, a dinner, and an optional dessert. The teacher may choose to dedicate a learning center to working on menu products or simply allow students time to work after other work is finished. When students complete the menu with this expectation, they have completed one activity from each content area, learning style, or level of Bloom's revised taxonomy, depending on the design of the menu.

- 1–2 days—The teacher chooses an activity or product from an objective to use with the entire class during that lesson time.

Suggested Forms

- All-purpose rubric

NUMBER WORDS

Directions: Choose one activity for breakfast and lunch.

Breakfast

Numbers and their names

My list of number words

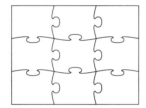

Numbers and number words

Lunch

15 number words

Number words from magazines

Writing words above 20

Directions: Choose one activity for dinner. After you are done with your dinner, you may do a dessert.

Dinner

 Counting by 10s to 100

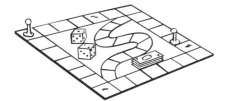 Playing with number words

 Your house with its address

Dessert

 Animals that teach number words

 Number words above 20

NUMBER WORDS

Directions: Choose one activity for breakfast and lunch.

Breakfast

Make a set of **concentration cards** to match numbers and their names.

Create a **list** of numbers and number words. Circle the longest one!

Design a **picture dictionary** to show 15 number words.

Lunch

Design a **collage** of number words that are found in magazines.

Create an **instruction card** for writing number words that are above 20.

Make a **drawing** of your house, and use number words to show the numbers in your address.

Directions: Choose one activity for dinner. After you are done with your dinner, you may do a dessert.

Dinner

 Write a **children's book** about animals that helps others learn their number words.

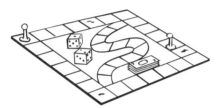 Create a **board game** that has players practice their number words.

 Make a **folded quiz book** to help others practice their number words above 20.

Dessert

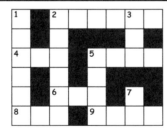 Make a **crossword puzzle** to practice writing number words.

 Number words follow a pattern once you get past 12. Why do you think this is? Does it happen in other languages as well? Research numbers in other languages and make a **poster** to share what you find.

NUMBER WORDS JIGSAW PUZZLE ▲

Directions: Write numbers and number words on the puzzle pieces. When the puzzle is put together, numbers and their words should match across the puzzle pieces. You may use this pattern or create your own jigsaw puzzle pieces.

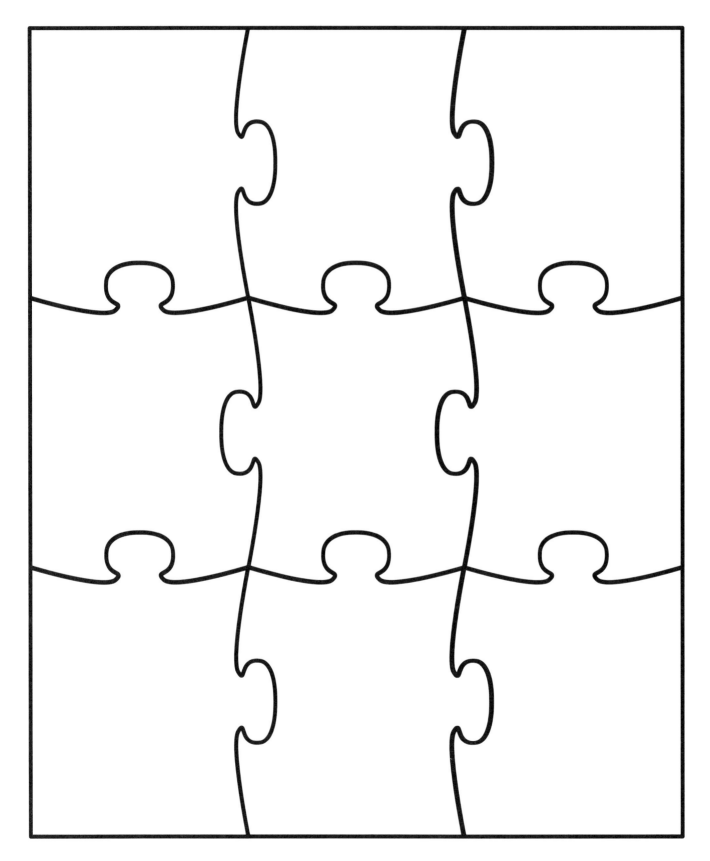

PLACE VALUE

GIVE ME 5 MENU ▲
AND 2-5-8 MENU ●

Objectives Covered Through This Menu and These Activities

- Students will demonstrate understanding of place value.
- Students will locate and designate place values in numbers.

Materials Needed by Students for Completion

- Poster board or large white paper
- Base ten blocks
- Blank index cards (for mobiles, concentration cards, and trading cards)
- Coat hangers (for mobiles)
- String (for mobiles)
- Newspapers or Sunday advertisements (for collages)

Special Notes on the Modifications of These Menus

- This topic includes two different types of menus: the Give Me 5 menu ▲ and the 2-5-8 menu ●. Although the primary modification on these two menus is the difference in point goal (5 ▲ vs. 10 ●), further modifications can be made based on the needs of your students. It is easy to modify each menu by simply changing the point goal; lowering the goal on each menu by 1 (or 2) may be more appropriate for some students. Students can color in the "extra" graphics on the bottom of the menu so that the colored graphics match the original goal of 5 or 10 points.

Special Notes on the Use of These Menus

- The lower level menu ▲ is specifically designed for students who are lower level readers or for those with a more limited vocabulary. It is meant to simply remind students of product options that have already been explained.

Time Frame

- 1 week—Students are given a menu as the unit is started, and the teacher discusses all of the product options on the menu. As the different options are discussed, students color or circle the graphic for each option that represents the activity they are most interested in completing so they meet their goal of 5 points (if using the Give Me 5 menu) or 10 points (if using the 2-5-8 menu). As students complete their products, they will color the corresponding graphics along the bottom of the menu so they can track their progress toward their point goal. As the lessons progress through the week, the teacher and students refer back to the menu options associated with the content being taught.

- 1–2 days—The teacher chooses an activity or product from the menu to use with the entire class.

Suggested Forms

- All-purpose rubric
- Free-choice proposal form (if appropriate for content and level of students) ●

PLACE VALUE

Directions: Choose activities from the menu below. The activities must total 5. Color or circle the picture next to each choice to show which activities you will complete. Color the circles along the bottom as you complete your activities to reach 5! All activities must be completed by _____.

2   Different place values

 5 place values

3  3-digit number

Place values for 1,586

5  Numbers and prices from newspaper

 Large numbers and their place values

PLACE VALUE

Directions: Choose activities from the menu below. The activities must total 10 points. Color or circle the picture next to each choice to show which activities you will complete. Color the circles along the bottom as you complete your activities to reach 10! All activities must be completed by _____.

2 Points

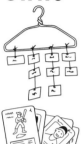

Make a **mobile** for a 3-digit number. Tell each number's place value and use base ten blocks to show the value of each digit in the number.

Create a set of **trading cards** for 5 different place values.

5 Points

Create an **advertisement** for a product that has 3 different place values in its price. Write the number and its values on the back of your advertisement.

Make a **collage** of numbers and prices found in newspapers. Label the different place values of each number or price.

Make a set of **concentration cards** to match large numbers with questions about their place values.

Free choice—Submit a proposal form to your teacher for a product of your choice.

8 Points

Write a **children's book** that uses food to teach place values.

Write and perform your own **song** to teach how to tell the difference between place values.

SKIP COUNTING

GIVE ME 5 MENU

Objectives Covered Through This Menu and These Activities

- Students will practice various forms of skip counting.

Materials Needed by Students for Completion

- Poster board or large white paper
- Large blank or lined index cards (for instruction cards)
- Blank index cards (for mobiles) ●
- Coat hangers (for mobiles) ●
- String (for mobiles) ●
- Materials for class game (folders, colored cards, etc.) ▲
- Materials for bulletin board displays ●

Special Notes on the Modifications of These Menus

- Because the Give Me 5 menu is a point-based menu, it is easy to modify by changing the point goal for those students for whom a goal of 5 may be too much. Lowering the goal on each menu by 1 (or 2) may be more appropriate for some students. Students can color in the "extra" graphics on the bottom of the menu so that the colored graphics match the original goal of 5 points.

Special Notes on the Use of These Menus

- The lower level menu ▲ is specifically designed for students who are lower level readers or for those with a more limited vocabulary. It is meant to simply remind students of product options that have already been explained.
- The on-level menu ● allows students to create a bulletin board display. Some classrooms may have only one bulletin board, so the teacher can divide the board into sections, or additional classroom wall or hall space can be sectioned off for the creation of these displays. Students can plan their displays based on the amount of space they are assigned.

Time Frame

- 1–3 days—Students are given a menu as the unit is started, and the teacher discusses all of the product options on the menu. As the different options are discussed, students color the graphic for each option that represents the activity they are most interested in completing so they meet their goal of 5 points. In this menu, that would imply students complete either two products (a 2-point and a 3-point) or one 5-point product. As students complete products, they will color the corresponding graphics along the bottom of the menu so they can track their progress toward their 5-point goal. As the lessons progress throughout the week, the teacher and students refer back to the menu options associated with the content being taught. The teacher may choose to dedicate a learning center to working on menu products or simply allow students time to work after other work is finished.
- 1 day—The teacher chooses an activity or product from the menu to use with the entire class.

Suggested Forms

- All-purpose rubric

SKIP COUNTING

Directions: Choose activities from the menu below. The activities must total 5. Color or circle the picture next to each choice to show which activities you will complete. Color the numbers along the bottom as you complete your activities to reach 5! All activities must be completed by _____.

2  Counting by 2s and 5s

 2s and 5s can be easy

3  2s, 5s, and 10s

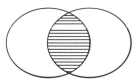 2s and 5s on a 100 chart

5  Odd-numbered things

 Skip counting dot-to-dot book with 5 pictures

1 2 3 4 5

SKIP COUNTING

Directions: Choose activities from the menu below. The activities must total 5. Color or circle the picture next to each choice to show which activities you will complete. Color the numbers along the bottom as you complete your activities to reach 5! All activities must be completed by _____.

2

Create an **instruction card** that shows how to count by 2s and 5s without using manipulatives.

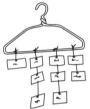

Make a **mobile** that shows how to count by 3s.

3

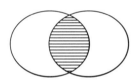

Using a 100 chart, count by 2s and color those squares red. Count by 5s and color those squares blue. Make a **Venn diagram** to show your results.

Create a **bulletin board display** that shows the patterns found in skip counting.

5

You only like even numbers and even-numbered things. Perform a **play** that shows all of the things you would not be able to do because you are picky about your numbers!

Make a dot-to-dot **children's book** that uses skip counting to make at least eight drawings. Use different kinds of skip counting, and include an answer key in your book.

1 2 3  5

GIVE ME 5   MATHEMATICAL SYMBOLS

GIVE ME 5 MENU ▲
AND 2-5-8 MENU ●

Objectives Covered Through This Menu and These Activities

- Students will correctly identify different mathematical symbols.
- Students will correctly use different mathematical symbols.

Materials Needed by Students for Completion

- Poster board or large white paper
- Blank index cards (for mobiles and trading cards)
- Coat hangers (for mobiles)
- String (for mobiles)
- Socks (for puppets)
- Paper bags (for puppets)
- Recycled materials (for puppets)
- Materials for class game (folders, colored cards, etc.) ●

Special Notes on the Modifications of These Menus

- This topic includes two different types of menus: the Give Me 5 menu ▲ and the 2-5-8 menu ●. Although the primary modification on these two menus is the difference in point goal (5 ▲ vs. 10 ●), further modifications can be made based on the needs of your students. It is easy to modify each menu by simply changing the point goal; lowering the goal on each menu by 1 (or 2) may be more appropriate for some students. Students can color in the "extra" graphics on the bottom of the menu so that the colored graphics match the original goal of 5 or 10 points.

Special Notes on the Use of These Menus

- The lower level menu ▲ is specifically designed for students who are lower level readers or for those with a more limited vocabulary. It is meant to simply remind students of product options that have already been explained.
- These menus ask students to use recycled materials to create their puppets. This does not mean only plastic and paper; instead, students

should focus on using materials in new ways. It works well if a box is started for "recycled" contributions at the beginning of the school year. That way, students always have access to these types of materials.

Time Frame

- 1 week—Students are given a menu as the unit is started, and the teacher discusses all of the product options on the menu. As the different options are discussed, students color or circle the graphic for each option that represents the activity they are most interested in completing so they meet their goal of 5 points (if using the Give Me 5 menu) or 10 points (if using the 2-5-8 menu). As students complete their products, they will color the corresponding graphics along the bottom of the menu so they can track their progress toward their point goal. As the lessons progress through the week, the teacher and students refer back to the menu options associated with the content being taught.
- 1–2 days—The teacher chooses an activity or product from the menu to use with the entire class.

Suggested Forms

- All-purpose rubric
- Free-choice proposal form (if appropriate for content and level of students) ●

MATHEMATICAL SYMBOLS

Directions: Choose activities from the menu below. The activities must total 5. Color or circle the picture next to each choice to show which activities you will complete. Color the symbols along the bottom as you complete your activities to reach 5! All activities must be completed by _____.

2

 Mathematical symbols

Symbols and their use

3

 Real-life mathematical symbols

 Mathematical symbols quiz

5

 Important symbols

 The best symbol

75

MATHEMATICAL SYMBOLS

Directions: Choose activities from the menu below. The activities must total 10 points. Color or circle the picture next to each choice to show which activities you will complete. Color the symbols along the bottom as you complete your activities to reach 10! All activities must be completed by _____.

2 Points

Make a **mobile** of the mathematical symbols with an example of how to use each one.

Create a set of **trading cards** for the mathematical symbols. Include examples of how each symbol is used.

5 Points

Create a **picture dictionary** for the mathematical symbols. Be sure to include examples.

Make a **folded quiz book** to test classmates on their knowledge of mathematical symbols.

Write and present a **play** that shows how important it is to choose the correct mathematical symbol. Include examples of how changing the symbol can have disastrous effects.

Free choice—Submit a proposal form to your teacher for a product of your choice.

8 Points

Design a **class game** in which your classmates have to guess the mathematical symbol based on the information you give.

Create a **puppet** for your favorite mathematical symbol using recycled materials. Perform a puppet show where your symbol talks about why it is the best symbol and what it does to numbers.

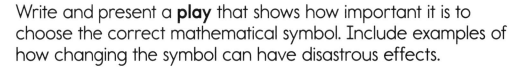

 **ODD AND EVEN NUMBERS**

GIVE ME 5 MENU

Objectives Covered Through This Menu and These Activities

- Students will distinguish odd from even numbers.
- Students will share different ways of identifying odd and even numbers.

Materials Needed by Students for Completion

- Poster board or large white paper
- Large blank or lined index cards (for instruction cards)
- Blank index cards (for mobiles and trading cards ●)
- Coat hangers (for mobiles)
- String (for mobiles)
- Paper bags (for puppets) ▲
- Socks (for puppets) ▲
- Recycled materials (for puppets) ▲
- DVD or VHS recorder (for commercials) ●

Special Notes on the Modifications of These Menus

- Because the Give Me 5 menu is a point-based menu, it is easy to modify by changing the point goal for those students for whom a goal of 5 may be too much. Lowering the goal on each menu by 1 (or 2) may be more appropriate for some students. Students can color in the "extra" graphics on the bottom of the menu so that the colored graphics match the original goal of 5 points.

Special Notes on the Use of These Menus

- The lower level menu ▲ is specifically designed for students who are lower level readers or for those with a more limited vocabulary. It is meant to simply remind students of product options that have already been explained.
- The lower level menu ▲ asks students to use recycled materials to create their puppets. This does not mean only plastic and paper; instead, students should focus on using materials in new ways. It works well if a box is started for "recycled" contributions at the beginning of the

school year. That way, students always have access to these types of materials.

- The on-level menu ⬤ gives students the opportunity to create a commercial. Although students enjoy producing their own videos, there are often difficulties obtaining the equipment and scheduling the use of a video recorder. This activity can be modified by allowing students to act out the commercial (like a play) or, if students have the technology, allowing them to produce a webcam version of their commercial.

Time Frame

- 1–3 days—Students are given a menu as the unit is started, and the teacher discusses all of the product options on the menu. As the different options are discussed, students color the graphic for each option that represents the activity they are most interested in completing so they meet their goal of 5 points. In this menu, that would imply students complete either two products (a 2-point and a 3-point) or one 5-point product. As students complete products, they will color the corresponding graphics along the bottom of the menu so they can track their progress toward their 5-point goal. As the lessons progress throughout the week, the teacher and students refer back to the menu options associated with the content being taught. The teacher may choose to dedicate a learning center to working on menu products or simply allow students time to work after other work is finished.
- 1 day—The teacher chooses an activity or product from the menu to use with the entire class.

Suggested Forms

- All-purpose rubric
- Free-choice proposal form (if appropriate for content and level of students) ⬤

ODD AND EVEN NUMBERS

Directions: Choose activities from the menu below. The activities must total 5. Color or circle the picture next to each choice to show which activities you will complete. Color the symbols along the bottom as you complete your activities to reach 5! All activities must be completed by _____.

2

 Odd and even numbers

 Objects that come in odds and evens

3

 How to tell if a number is odd or even

 Odd number of parts

5

 Do you like odd or even numbers?

Are odd or even numbers better?

ODD AND EVEN NUMBERS

Directions: Choose activities from the menu below. The activities must total 5. Color or circle the picture next to each choice to show which activities you will complete. Color the symbols along the bottom as you complete your activities to reach 5! All activities must be completed by _____.

2

Make a set of **trading cards** for 3 even numbers and 3 odd numbers.

Create an odd and even **mobile** with pictures of objects that come in odd numbers and even numbers.

3

Write an **instruction card** that helps a student tell if a number is odd or even.

Create a **folded quiz book** about odd and even numbers.

5

Scientists say that nature is full of more odd numbers than even ones. Write a **children's book** that shows examples of this.

Do you prefer odd or even numbers? Create a **commercial** for the type of numbers you like better. Include examples of and reasons for your choice in your commercial.

Free choice—Submit a proposal form to your teacher for a product of your choice.

 **100TH DAY OF SCHOOL**

GIVE ME 5 MENU ▲
AND 2-5-8 MENU ●

Objectives Covered Through This Menu and These Activities

- Students will practice counting to 100.
- Students will identify 100 objects found around them.

Materials Needed by Students for Completion

- Poster board or large white paper
- Socks (for puppets) ▲
- Paper bags (for puppets) ▲
- Recycled materials (for puppets) ▲
- Blank index cards (for mobiles) ●
- Coat hangers (for mobiles) ●
- String (for mobiles) ●
- 100th Day of School Cube template
- Plastic bags for collections

Special Notes on the Modifications of These Menus

- This topic includes two different types of menus: the Give Me 5 menu ▲ and the 2-5-8 menu ●. Although the primary modification on these two menus is the difference in point goal (5 ▲ vs. 10 ●), further modifications can be made based on the needs of your students. It is easy to modify each menu by simply changing the point goal; lowering the goal on each menu by 1 (or 2) may be more appropriate for some students. Students can color in the "extra" graphics on the bottom of the menu so that the colored graphics match the original goal of 5 or 10 points.

Special Notes on the Use of These Menus

- The lower level menu ▲ is specifically designed for students who are lower level readers or for those with a more limited vocabulary. It is meant to simply remind students of product options that have already been explained.

- The lower level menu ▲ asks students to use recycled materials to create their puppets. This does not mean only plastic and paper; instead, students should focus on using materials in new ways. It works well if a box is started for "recycled" contributions at the beginning of the school year. That way, students always have access to these types of materials.

Time Frame

- 1 week—Students are given a menu as the unit is started, and the teacher discusses all of the product options on the menu. As the different options are discussed, students color or circle the graphic for each option that represents the activity they are most interested in completing so they meet their goal of 5 points (if using the Give Me 5 menu) or 10 points (if using the 2-5-8 menu). As students complete their products, they will color the corresponding graphics along the bottom of the menu so they can track their progress toward their point goal. As the lessons progress through the week, the teacher and students refer back to the menu options associated with the content being taught.
- 1–2 days—The teacher chooses an activity or product from the menu to use with the entire class.

Suggested Forms

- All-purpose rubric
- Free-choice proposal form (if appropriate for content and level of students) ●

100TH DAY OF SCHOOL

Directions: Choose activities from the menu below. The activities must total 5. Color or circle the picture next to each choice to show which activities you will complete. Color the calendars along the bottom as you complete your activities to reach 5! All activities must be completed by _____.

2  100 things in a small plastic bag

 Groups larger than 100

3 Activities for 100th day

 Happy 100th day!

5  100 things you did today

 The best 100th day

100TH DAY OF SCHOOL

Directions: Choose activities from the menu below. The activities must total 10 points. Color or circle the picture next to each choice to show which activities you will complete. Color the calendars along the bottom as you complete your activities to reach 10! All activities must be completed by _____.

2 Points

Create a **collection** of 100 things that can fit into a small plastic bag.

Make a **mobile** to show different things that total 100 when counted together.

5 Points

Create an **advertisement** to show why the 100th day of school is special. (Include 100 items on your ad!)

Create a **cube** with different activities that you could do to celebrate the 100th day of school.

Create a **greeting card** to celebrate the 100th day of school. Include 100 items or decorations on the card.

Free choice—Submit a proposal form to your teacher for a product of your choice.

8 Points

Make a plan for your 100th day of school in which you will do exactly 100 things. Write a **diary** about the 100 things you did.

Write a **newspaper article** that tells others about the 100th day of school and why it is special to you and your school.

100TH DAY OF SCHOOL CUBE

Directions: Choose your favorite living things. Draw or glue pictures on each side. Use this pattern or create your own cube.

At School

At Home

With My Friends

Alone

Outside

I would most like to . . .

GIVE ME 5 — GREATER THAN, LESS THAN

GIVE ME 5 MENU

Objectives Covered Through This Menu and These Activities

- Students will write number sentences showing greater than and less than relationships.

Materials Needed by Students for Completion

- Poster board or large white paper
- Magazines (for collages)
- Blank index cards (for concentration cards)
- Materials for class game (folders, colored cards, etc.) ●

Special Notes on the Modifications of These Menus

- Because the Give Me 5 menu is a point-based menu, it is easy to modify by changing the point goal for those students for whom a goal of 5 may be too much. Lowering the goal on each menu by 1 (or 2) may be more appropriate for some students. Students can color in the "extra" graphics on the bottom of the menu so that the colored graphics match the original goal of 5 points.

Special Notes on the Use of These Menus

- The lower level menu ▲ is specifically designed for students who are lower level readers or for those with a more limited vocabulary. It is meant to simply remind students of product options that have already been explained.
- The on-level menu ● gives students the opportunity to demonstrate a concept. This can take a significant amount of time and organization. It can save time if the demonstration is recorded to share at a later time or if all of the students who choose to do a demonstration sign up for a designated day and time.

Time Frame

- 1–3 days—Students are given a menu as the unit is started, and the teacher discusses all of the product options on the menu. As the different options are discussed, students color the graphic for each option that represents the activity they are most interested in completing so they meet their goal of 5 points. In this menu, that would imply students complete either two products (a 2-point and a 3-point) or one 5-point product. As students complete products, they will color the corresponding graphics along the bottom of the menu so they can track their progress toward their 5-point goal. As the lessons progress throughout the week, the teacher and students refer back to the menu options associated with the content being taught. The teacher may choose to dedicate a learning center to working on menu products or simply allow students time to work after other work is finished.

- 1 day—The teacher chooses an activity or product from the menu to use with the entire class.

Suggested Forms

- All-purpose rubric

GREATER THAN, LESS THAN

Directions: Choose activities from the menu below. The activities must total 5. Color or circle the picture next to each choice to show which activities you will complete. Color the greater than and less than symbols along the bottom as you complete your activities to reach 5! All activities must be completed by

_____.

2  Greater than or less than?

 Symbols in pictures

3  3 greater than or less than sentences

 Greater than and less than number sentences

5  Using greater than and less than symbols

Learning about greater than and less than

GREATER THAN, LESS THAN

Directions: Choose activities from the menu below. The activities must total 5. Color or circle the picture next to each choice to show which activities you will complete. Color the greater than and less than symbols along the bottom as you complete your activities to reach 5! All activities must be completed by

_____.

2

Write 3 sentences that use the terms greater than or less than. Make each word sentence into a number sentence.

Create a **collage** with pictures that look like greater than and less than symbols. Label each symbol in its picture.

3

Write and sing a **song** to teach your classmates about greater than and less than.

Make a set of **concentration cards** to match greater than and less than number sentences with word sentences.

5

Create a **class game** in which players guess if the number of something is greater than or less than 10. Include an answer key for your game.

Do a **demonstration** that shows how to use the greater than and less than symbols correctly in a number sentence with more than 2 numbers.

PATTERNS

GIVE ME 5 MENU ▲
AND 2-5-8 MENU ●

Objectives Covered Through This Menu and These Activities

- Students will sort, classify, and order objects by size, number, and other properties.
- Students will recognize, describe, and extend patterns, such as sequences of sounds and shapes or simple numeric patterns, and translate from one representation to another.
- Students will analyze how both repeating and growing patterns are generated.

Materials Needed by Students for Completion

- Poster board or large white paper
- Blank index cards (for concentration ● and trading cards)
- Magazines (for collages)
- Materials for bulletin board displays ●
- Materials for board games (folders, colored cards, etc.)

Special Notes on the Modifications of These Menus

- This topic includes two different types of menus: the Give Me 5 menu ▲ and the 2-5-8 menu ●. Although the primary modification on these two menus is the difference in point goal (5 ▲ vs. 10 ●), further modifications can be made based on the needs of your students. It is easy to modify each menu by simply changing the point goal; lowering the goal on each menu by 1 (or 2) may be more appropriate for some students. Students can color in the "extra" graphics on the bottom of the menu so that the colored graphics match the original goal of 5 or 10 points.

Special Notes on the Use of These Menus

- The lower level menu ▲ is specifically designed for students who are lower level readers or for those with a more limited vocabulary. It is meant to simply remind students of product options that have already been explained.

- The on-level menu ● allows students to create a bulletin board display. Some classrooms may have only one bulletin board, so the teacher can divide the board into sections, or additional classroom wall or hall space can be sectioned off for the creation of these displays. Students can plan their displays based on the amount of space they are assigned.

Time Frame

- 1 week—Students are given a menu as the unit is started, and the teacher discusses all of the product options on the menu. As the different options are discussed, students color or circle the graphic for each option that represents the activity they are most interested in completing so they meet their goal of 5 points (if using the Give Me 5 menu) or 10 points (if using the 2-5-8 menu). As students complete their products, they will color the corresponding graphics along the bottom of the menu so they can track their progress toward their point goal. As the lessons progress through the week, the teacher and students refer back to the menu options associated with the content being taught.
- 1–2 days—The teacher chooses an activity or product from the menu to use with the entire class.

Suggested Forms

- All purpose rubric

PATTERNS

Directions: Choose activities from the menu below. The activities must total 5. Color or circle the picture next to each choice to show which activities you will complete. Color the checkerboards along the bottom as you complete your activities to reach 5! All activities must be completed by _____.

2

4 patterns in the classroom

A repeating pattern

3

3 ways to sort

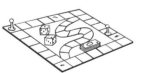

Cards for your favorite animals

5

Patterns of shapes

Patterns in nature

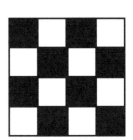

Name:_____ ●

PATTERNS

Directions: Choose activities from the menu below. The activities must total 10 points. Color or circle the picture next to each choice to show which activities you will complete. Color the checkerboards along the bottom as you complete your activities to reach 10! All activities must be completed by _____.

2 Points

Make a **collection** of at least 20 different items. Show at least 3 different ways you could sort your collection and how your collection would look if it were sorted each way.

Develop a set of **trading cards** about your favorite animals. Come up with 2 different ways you could sort the cards. Write a sentence explaining why you chose to sort them that way.

5 Points

Create a set of **concentration cards**. Each pair should have a number pattern on one of the cards and the next number in the series on the other card. Include an answer key.

Develop a **bulletin board display** that shows different ways of sorting classroom objects.

Create a **board game** that has players try to figure out number patterns.

Make a **collage** that has a repeating pattern. Be creative in what pattern you choose!

8 Points

Write a **children's book** about patterns we see in nature. Include lots of pictures as examples!

Your teacher has decided that there will be homework every other day, starting today. Construct a plan that shows how many days you will have homework this week. Can you predict how many days you will have homework this month? This year? Show your predictions on a **poster**.

MONEY

MEAL MENU

Objectives Covered Through This Menu and These Activities

- Students will describe the different coins and bills in the United States currency system.
- Students will express various uses for money, from spending to saving.

Materials Needed by Students for Completion

- Poster board or large white paper
- Scrapbooking materials
- Blank index cards (for concentration cards and mobiles)
- Coat hangers (for mobiles)
- String (for mobiles)
- Socks (for puppets)
- Paper bags (for puppets)
- Recycled materials (for puppets)
- Scrapbooking materials
- Microsoft PowerPoint or other slideshow software ●
- Money Cube template
- Money Jigsaw Puzzle template ▲
- Materials for board games (folders, colored cards, etc.)

Special Notes on the Modifications of These Menus

- The Meal menu format has a design feature that makes it easy to reduce the number of choices students face at one time. Students can be given the left side (breakfast and lunch, or lower levels of thinking) as their first options. After these two meal products have been completed, students can then receive the right side (dinner and dessert, or higher levels of thinking and enrichment options). After becoming accustomed to the amount of choice, students can then get the entire meal menu at once.

Special Notes on the Use of These Menus

- The lower level menu ▲ is specifically designed for students who are lower level readers or for those with a more limited vocabulary. It is

meant to simply remind students of product options that have already been explained.

- These menus ask students to use recycled materials to create their puppets. This does not mean only plastic and paper; instead, students should focus on using materials in new ways. It works well if a box is started for "recycled" contributions at the beginning of the school year. That way, students always have access to these types of materials.

Time Frame

- 1 week—Students are given a menu as the unit is started. As the unit progresses throughout the week, students should refer back to the menu options associated with that content. The teacher will go over all of the options for that content and have students color or circle the graphic for each option that represents the activity they are most interested in completing. As teaching continues, the activities chosen and completed should create a full day's meal, with a breakfast, a lunch, a dinner, and an optional dessert. The teacher may choose to dedicate a learning center to working on menu products or simply allow students time to work after other work is finished. When students complete the menu with this expectation, they have completed one activity from each content area, learning style, or level of Bloom's revised taxonomy, depending on the design of the menu.
- 1–2 days—The teacher chooses an activity or product from an objective to use with the entire class during that lesson time.

Suggested Forms

- All-purpose rubric

MONEY

Directions: Choose one activity for breakfast and lunch.

Breakfast

Our money and its value

Our coins and their values

Paper money and coins

Lunch

The ant or the grasshopper?

What do we need?

Why should people save money?

Directions: Choose one activity for dinner. After you are done with your dinner, you may do a dessert.

Dinner

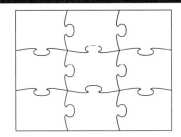 Buying something

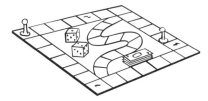 Money game

 Spending $1, $10, and $100

Dessert

 Spending $1,000

 Making money

MONEY

Directions: Choose one activity for breakfast and lunch.

Breakfast

Construct a **mobile** that shows our money and its values.

Create a set of **concentration cards** for our coins and their values.

Read a library book about money. Design a new **book cover** for the book you chose.

Lunch

Read the fable of the ant and the grasshopper. Create a **puppet** for one of the characters and retell the fable using money instead of food.

Design a **cube** showing six different items that people *need* to spend money on.

Create a **song** about the importance of saving money.

Directions: Choose one activity for dinner. After you are done with your dinner, you may do a dessert.

Dinner

 Create a **children's book** that teaches about our money and how people use it.

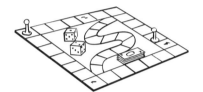 Design your own money **board game** in which players make choices about buying items.

 Make a **scrapbook** of items you could buy with $0.50, $1, $10, and $100.

Dessert

  Research a money system used in another country. Design a **PowerPoint presentation** showing that country's system and comparing it to ours.

 If you had $1,000, what would you buy? Make a **poster** with pictures of everything you would buy and include the prices.

MONEY CUBE

Directions: There are lots of things that people buy. Some things they need; others they want. Think about things that people need and draw a picture of the six most important things people buy. Use this pattern or create your own cube.

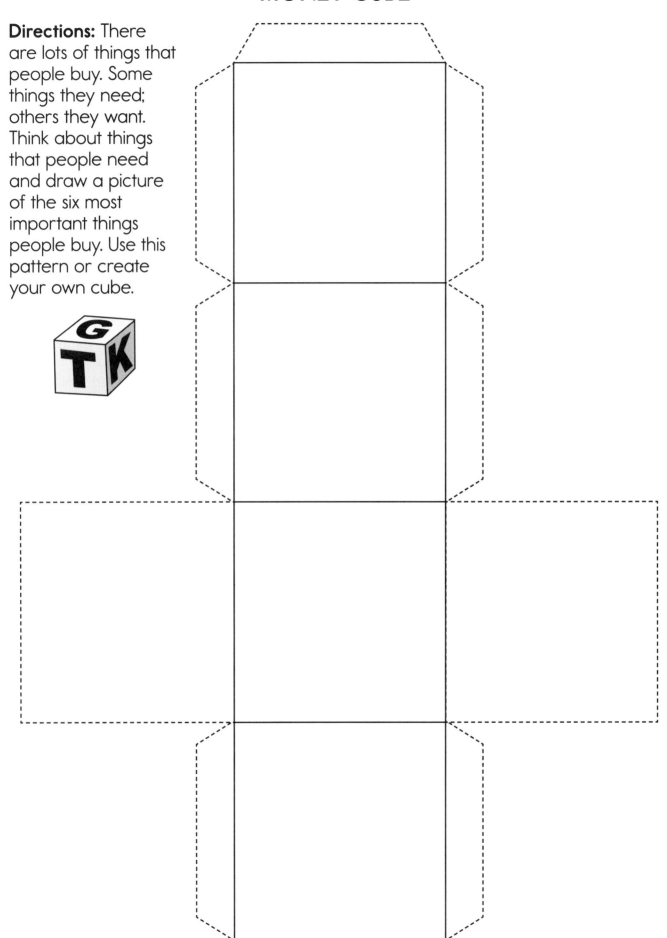

MONEY JIGSAW PUZZLE

Directions: Draw things families need money to buy. When the puzzle is put together, it should make a picture of things that a family may need to buy. You may use this pattern or create your own jigsaw puzzle pieces.

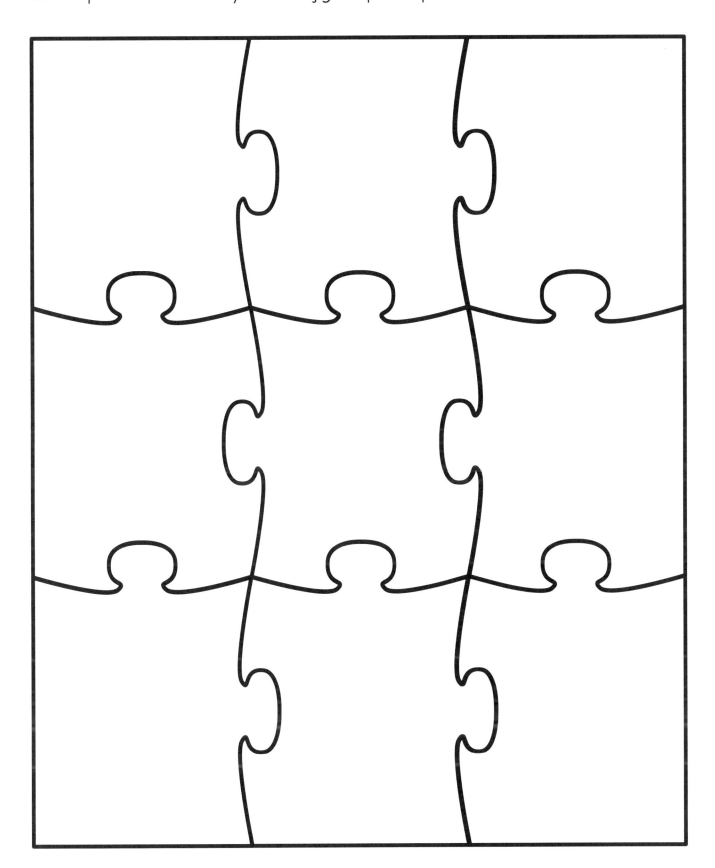

CHAPTER 6

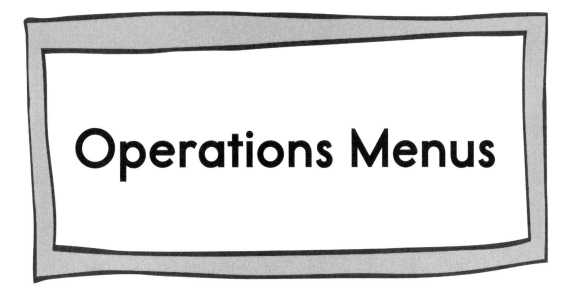

Operations Menus

ADDITION

THREE-SHAPE MENU

Objectives Covered Through This Menu and These Activities

- Students will develop and use strategies for whole-number addition.
- Students will use a variety of computation methods and tools, including objects, paper and pencils, and calculators.

Materials Needed by Students for Completion

- Poster board or large white paper
- Blank index cards (for concentration cards)
- Large blank or lined index cards (for instruction cards) ▲
- Materials for models ●
- Recycled materials (for models) ●
- Materials for board games (folders, colored cards, etc.)

Special Notes on the Modifications of These Menus

- These two Three-Shape menus have slightly different formats. The lower level menu ▲ has a dotted line with separate instructions for each section. This visually separates the page beyond just the different shapes. This also makes it easy for the teacher to cut the menu as needed based on the comfort level of the students when it comes to choice. If it is the first time choice is being introduced, the children may receive only the strip of square options. Then when they have finished, they can receive the circles and then the diamonds. After students are more accustomed to options, the menu might be cut just once after the circles, so students can select a square and a circle and submit them to the teacher. Then they can choose from the diamond strip they receive. The ultimate goal would be to work up to allowing students to have all nine options at once and not be overwhelmed. The on-level menu ● has one dotted line separating the diamonds from the rest of the menu, making the enrichment options easy to include or cut and distribute later at the teacher's discretion.

Special Notes on the Use of These Menus

- The lower level menu ▲ is specifically designed for students who are lower level readers or for those with a more limited vocabulary. It is meant to simply remind students of product options that have already been explained.
- The on-level menu ● asks students to use recycled materials to create their models. This does not mean only plastic and paper; instead, students should focus on using materials in new ways. It works well if a box is started for "recycled" contributions at the beginning of the school year. That way, students always have access to these types of materials.

Time Frame

- 1–2 weeks—Students are given a menu as the unit is started. As the unit progresses throughout the week, students should refer back to the menu options associated with that content. The teacher will go over all of the options for that content and have students circle the items that represent the activities they are most interested in completing. As teaching continues over the next 1–2 weeks, shapes will be colored in as each activity is completed. The activities should be completed in such a way that students complete one from each shape group. When students complete this pattern, they will have completed one activity from each content area, learning style, or level of Bloom's revised taxonomy, depending on the design of the menu.
- 1–2 days—The teacher chooses an activity or product from an objective to use with the entire class during that lesson time.

Suggested Forms

- All-purpose rubric

ADDITION

Directions: Pick a square. Circle it. Color in the square when you are done.

5 word problems 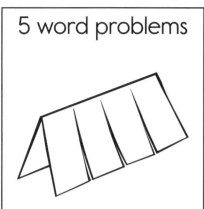	**Addition problems and answers** 	**3 hard addition problems** 

Directions: Pick a circle. Circle it. Color in the circle when you are done.

Practicing addition problems

Adding numbers

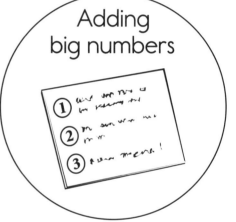

Adding big numbers

Directions: Pick a diamond. Circle it. Color in the diamond when you are done.

Trouble adding numbers

Adding distances

Machine answers addition problems

Name:_____

ADDITION

Directions: Pick a square. Circle it. Color in the square when you are done.

| Make a **folded quiz book** with 8 different addition word problems on it. Include an answer key.  | Make a set of **concentration cards** with an addition problem on one card and the answer on the other. | Design a **poster** to explain how to do an addition problem using pictures. |

Directions: Pick a circle. Circle it. Color in the circle when you are done.

Create **a board game** in which players have to answer addition problems as they progress through the game.

Perform **a song** about adding that includes at least two different word problems and how to solve them.

Make **a model** that your classmates could use to show they understand how to add numbers.

Directions: Pick a diamond. Circle it. Color in the diamond when you are done.

Write **a story** about a child who is having trouble adding numbers and what he or she does to learn.

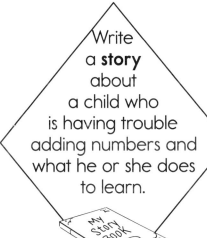

Create **a class game** to help your classmates practice answering addition word problems.

Develop an **advertisement** for a machine that will answer addition problems. It will only do addition. Include how the machine works in your advertisement.

SUBTRACTION

THREE-SHAPE MENU ▲
AND POINT-BASED LIST MENU ●

Objectives Covered Through This Menu and These Activities

- Students will understand the effects of subtracting whole numbers.
- Students will complete basic subtraction problems, including regrouping when appropriate.

Materials Needed by Students for Completion

- Poster board or large white paper
- Blank index cards (for concentration cards)
- Socks (for puppets)
- Paper bags (for puppets)
- Recycled materials (for puppets and models)
- Materials for bulletin board display ●
- Materials for board games (folders, colored cards, etc.)

Special Notes on the Modifications of These Menus

- This topic includes two different types of menus: the Three-Shape menu ▲ and the Point-Based List menu ●. The Three-Shape menu is specifically selected for the lower level option as it easily allows the menu to be broken into manageable bits. The menu itself can be cut along the dotted lines into strips of the same shape. Students can then be given a strip of square product choices for their use. Once they have chosen and submitted that product for grading, they can be given the circle strip, and finally the diamond strip. Because this type of menu is designed to become more advanced as students move through the shapes, teachers may choose to provide their lower level students with the top two shapes and save the diamonds for enrichment. The Point-Based List menu was selected not just because of its ease of modification but also to reinforce the topic of subtraction. This menu format can be modified by increasing or decreasing the target number of points a student needs to complete; simply fill in the goal at the bottom of the menu.

Special Notes on the Use of These Menus

- These menus ask students to use recycled materials to create their puppets and models. This does not mean only plastic and paper; instead, students should focus on using materials in new ways. It works well if a box is started for "recycled" contributions at the beginning of the school year. That way, students always have access to these types of materials.
- The on-level menu ● allows students to create a bulletin board display. Some classrooms may have only one bulletin board, so the teacher can divide the board into sections, or additional classroom wall or hall space can be sectioned off for the creation of these displays. Students can plan their displays based on the amount of space they are assigned.

Time Frame

- 1–2 weeks—Students are given a menu as the unit is started and the target goal (one product from each shape if using the Three-Shape menu ▲ or the point goal if using the Point-Based List menu ●) is discussed. The teacher will go over all of the options on the menu and have students select the activities they are most interested in completing. If students are using the Point-Based List menu ●, teachers will also need to set aside a few moments to sign the agreement at the bottom of the page with each student; this is not necessary with the Three-Shape menu ▲. As the unit progresses, students should refer back to the menu options associated with that content; activities are completed by students and submitted for grading. The teacher may choose to dedicate a learning center to working on menu products or simply allow students time to work after other work is finished.
- 1–2 days—The teacher chooses an activity or product from an objective to use with the entire class during that lesson time.

Suggested Forms

- All-purpose rubric
- Free-choice proposal form (if appropriate for content and level of students) ●

SUBTRACTION

Directions: Pick a square. Circle it. Color in the square when you are done.

Words that mean subtract 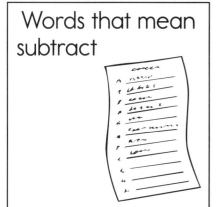	Showing how to subtract 	Solving a subtraction problem 

Directions: Pick a circle. Circle it. Color in the circle when you are done.

3 different subtraction word problems with answers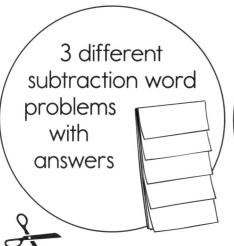

Matching subtraction problems with their answers

Starts at 50 and the first person to reach zero wins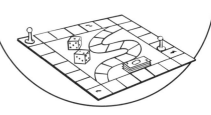

Directions: Pick a diamond. Circle it. Color in the diamond when you are done.

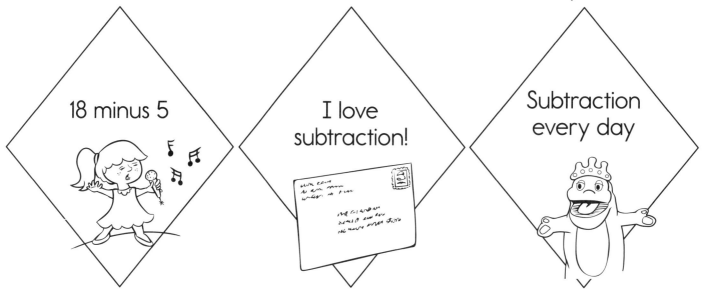

18 minus 5

I love subtraction!

Subtraction every day

Name:_____

SUBTRACTION

Directions:
1. You may complete as many of the activities listed as you can within the time period.
2. You may choose any combination of activities. Your goal is 20 points.
3. You must share your plan with your teacher by _____.
4. Activities may be turned in at any time during the working time period. They will be graded and recorded on this sheet as you continue to work, so keep it safe!

Plan to Do	Activity to Complete	Point Value	Date Completed	Points Earned
	Create a **model** that shows how subtraction works.	5		
	List all of the different words used in word problems to mean subtract.	5		
	Design a **folded quiz book** with at least 5 different subtraction word problems. Don't forget the answer key!	5		
	Construct a set of **concentration cards** in which players match subtraction problems with their answers.	5		
	Create a **song** about 21 minus 7.	10		
	Write a **children's book** about subtraction and how to solve subtraction problems.	10		
	Create a **bulletin board display** that another teacher could use to teach the basics of subtraction.	10		
	Construct a **puppet** out of recycled materials to use in a puppet show that shows that subtraction happens every day—and not always in math problems!	15		
	Develop a subtraction **board game** in which everyone starts with the number 100, and the first person to reach zero wins!	15		
	Free choice—Submit a proposal form to your teacher for a product of your choice.	5–15		
	Total number of points you are planning to earn:	**Total points earned:**		

I am planning to complete _____ activities, which could earn up to a total of _____ points.

Teacher's initials _____ Student's signature _____

BASIC ADDITION
AND SUBTRACTION

THREE-SHAPE MENU

Objectives Covered Through This Menu and These Activities

- Students will show the processes of addition and subtraction both in words and with pictures.
- Students will understand how addition and subtraction are related.
- Students will use addition and subtraction to solve word problems.
- Students will identify various fact families.

Materials Needed by Students for Completion

- Poster board or large white paper
- Large blank or lined index cards (for instruction cards)
- Blank index cards (for mobiles and concentration cards)
- Coat hangers (for mobiles)
- String (for mobiles)
- Microsoft PowerPoint or other slideshow software ●
- Word Problem Cube template
- Materials for board games (folders, colored cards, etc.)

Special Notes on the Modifications of These Menus

- These two Three-Shape menus have slightly different formats. The lower level menu ▲ has a dotted line with separate instructions for each section. This visually separates the page beyond just the different shapes. This also makes it easy for the teacher to cut the menu as needed based on the comfort level of the students when it comes to choice. If it is the first time choice is being introduced, the children may receive only the strip of square options. Then when they have finished, they can receive the circles and then the diamonds. After students are more accustomed to options, the menu might be cut just once after the circles, so students can select a square and a circle and submit them to the teacher. Then they can choose from the diamond strip they receive. The ultimate goal would be to work up to allowing students to have all nine options at once and not be overwhelmed. The on-level menu ● has one dotted line separating the diamonds from the rest of the menu, making the enrichment options easy to include or cut and distribute later at the teacher's discretion.

Special Notes on the Use of These Menus

- The lower level menu ▲ is specifically designed for students who are lower level readers or for those with a more limited vocabulary. It is meant to simply remind students of product options that have already been explained.
- These menus give students the opportunity to demonstrate a concept. This can take a significant amount of time and organization. It can save time if the demonstration is recorded to share at a later time or if all of the students who choose to do a demonstration sign up for a designated day and time.

Time Frame

- 1–2 weeks—Students are given a menu as the unit is started. As the unit progresses throughout the week, students should refer back to the menu options associated with that content. The teacher will go over all of the options for that content and have students circle the items that represent the activities they are most interested in completing. As teaching continues over the next 1–2 weeks, shapes will be colored in as each activity is completed. The activities should be completed in such a way that students complete one from each shape group. When students complete this pattern, they will have completed one activity from each content area, learning style, or level of Bloom's revised taxonomy, depending on the design of the menu.
- 1–2 days—The teacher chooses an activity or product from an objective to use with the entire class during that lesson time.

Suggested Forms

- All-purpose rubric

BASIC ADDITION AND SUBTRACTION

Directions: Pick a square. Circle it. Color in the square when you are done.

Adding and subtracting using words 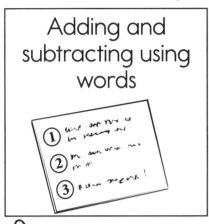	3 different fact families 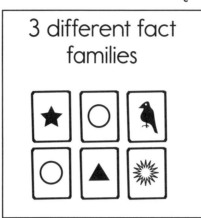	How to add and subtract 

- -

Directions: Pick a circle. Circle it. Color in the circle when you are done.

3 addition and 3 subtraction word problems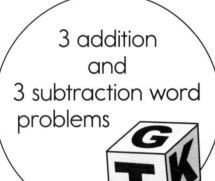

Practicing addition and subtraction word problems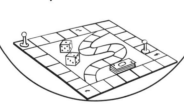

3 word problems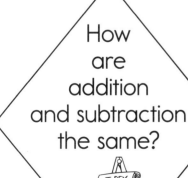

- -

Directions: Pick a diamond. Circle it. Color in the diamond when you are done.

How are addition and subtraction the same?

Compare and contrast addition and subtraction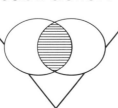

If you know how to add, you can subtract!

BASIC ADDITION AND SUBTRACTION

Directions: Pick a square. Circle it. Color in the square when you are done.

Write an **instruction card** that shows the processes of addition and subtraction using pictures and words. 	Do a **demonstration** that shows how addition and subtraction are related. Be sure to include at least two examples.	Develop a set of **concentration cards** to match addition and subtraction problems that are part of the same fact family.

Directions: Pick a circle. Circle it. Color in the circle when you are done.

Make a **cube** with a different word problem on each side. 3 of the problems should use addition, and 3 should use subtraction.

Create a **board game** where players use addition and subtraction word problems to move forward. Include an answer key.

Using a magazine, find at least 3 pictures. Make up a word problem for each picture. Create a **mobile** of the pictures and the word problems.

Directions: Pick a diamond. Circle it. Color in the diamond when you are done.

Make a **PowerPoint presentation** to show the processes of addition and subtraction using graphics.

Sing a **song** that tells how addition is like subtraction.

Make a **Venn diagram** to compare and contrast addition and subtraction.

WORD PROBLEM CUBE

Directions: Make a cube with a different word problem on each side. Three of the problems should use addition to solve them and 3 should use subtraction. Use this pattern or create your own cube.

Addition

Addition

Subtraction	Addition	Subtraction

Subtraction

THE GROCERY STORE

MEAL MENU

Objectives Covered Through This Menu and These Activities

- Students will understand that money is used to purchase grocery items.
- Students will investigate how to get the most for their money.
- Students will use mathematical functions to solve money-related problems.

Materials Needed by Students for Completion

- Poster board or large white paper
- Advertisements from a grocery store
- Library books about children and money
- Socks (for puppets)
- Paper bags (for puppets)
- Recycled materials (for models and puppets)
- Scrapbooking materials ●
- Materials for board games (folders, colored cards, etc.)
- Magazines (for collages)
- DVD or VHS recorder (for commercial) ▲
- Materials for bulletin board displays

Special Notes on the Modifications of These Menus

- The Meal menu format has a design feature that makes it easy to reduce the number of choices students face at one time. Students can be given the left side (breakfast and lunch, or lower levels of thinking) as their first options. After these two meal products have been completed, students can then receive the right side (dinner and dessert, or higher levels of thinking and enrichment options). After becoming accustomed to the amount of choice, students can then get the entire meal menu at once.

Special Notes on the Use of These Menus

- The lower level menu ▲ is specifically designed for students who are lower level readers or for those with a more limited vocabulary. It is meant to simply remind students of product options that have already been explained.
- The lower level menu ▲ gives students the opportunity to create a commercial. Although students enjoy producing their own videos, there are often difficulties obtaining the equipment and scheduling the use of a video recorder. This activity can be modified by allowing students to act out the commercial (like a play) or, if students have the technology, allowing them to produce a webcam version of their commercial.
- These menus ask students to use recycled materials to create their puppets and models. This does not mean only plastic and paper; instead, students should focus on using materials in new ways. It works well if a box is started for "recycled" contributions at the beginning of the school year. That way, students always have access to these types of materials.
- These menus allow students to create a bulletin board display. Some classrooms may have only one bulletin board, so the teacher can divide the board into sections, or additional classroom wall or hall space can be sectioned off for the creation of these displays. Students can plan their displays based on the amount of space they are assigned.

Time Frame

- 1 week—Students are given a menu as the unit is started. As the unit progresses throughout the week, students should refer back to the menu options associated with that content. The teacher will go over all of the options for that content and have students color or circle the graphic for each option that represents the activity they are most interested in completing. As teaching continues, the activities chosen and completed should create a full day's meal, with a breakfast, a lunch, a dinner, and an optional dessert. The teacher may choose to dedicate a learning center to working on menu products or simply allow students time to work after other work is finished. When students complete the menu with this expectation, they have completed one activity from each content area, learning style, or level of Bloom's revised taxonomy, depending on the design of the menu.

- 1–2 days—The teacher chooses an activity or product from an objective to use with the entire class during that lesson time.

Suggested Forms

- All-purpose rubric

THE GROCERY STORE

Directions: Choose one activity for breakfast and lunch.

Breakfast

Types of things at a grocery store

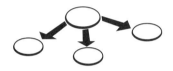

Areas of a grocery store

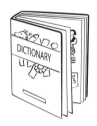

Names of the grocery store aisles

Lunch

At least 5 items, spending less than $10

Using an advertisement to make math questions

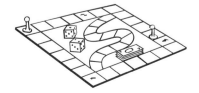

Trip through the grocery store

Directions: Choose one activity for dinner. After you are done with your dinner, you may do a dessert.

Dinner

 Being a good shopper

 Saving money at the grocery store

 Ways to spend less

Dessert

 My perfect grocery store

 The best grocery store in my town

THE GROCERY STORE

Directions: Choose one activity for breakfast and lunch.

Breakfast

Create a **collage** of the different types of things you can buy at a grocery store.

Make a **mind map** for the major areas of a grocery store and what is found in each area.

Go on a field trip to your grocery store and create a **map** of the store.

Lunch

Using an advertisement from your local grocery store, create a **poster** of how you would spend $10. You need to buy at least 7 items.

Design a **bulletin board display** asking math questions about an advertisement from your local grocery store.

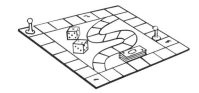

Develop a **board game** in which players answer math questions using an advertisement from your local grocery store.

Directions: Choose one activity for dinner. After you are done with your dinner, you may do a dessert.

Dinner

Create a **puppet** out of recycled materials that wants to tell others about how to be a good shopper at the grocery store. Include examples!

Design a **children's book** that shows how to save money at the grocery store.

Find out different ways to save money at the grocery store and make a **scrapbook** of items that can help others spend less while shopping.

Dessert

Read a library book about children and money. Design a **brochure** about the tips presented in the book.

Using recycled materials, make a **model** of your perfect grocery store. What types of products would it carry, and how would it be arranged?

CHAPTER 7

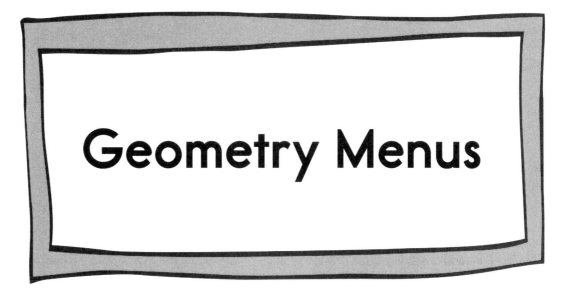

Geometry Menus

BASIC SHAPES

THREE-SHAPE MENU ▲
AND TIC-TAC-TOE MENU ●

Objectives Covered Through This Menu and These Activities

- Students will identify basic shapes.
- Students will use basic shapes in creative ways.

Materials Needed by Students for Completion

- Poster board or large white paper
- Blank index cards (for mobiles)
- Coat hangers (for mobiles)
- String (for mobiles)
- Paper bags (for puppets) ●
- Socks (for puppets) ●
- Recycled materials (for puppets) ●
- Magazines (for collages)
- Materials for board games (folders, colored cards, etc.)
- *The Missing Piece* by Shel Silverstein ●
- Shoeboxes (for mystery objects) ▲

Special Notes on the Modifications of These Menus

- This topic has two different menu formats: the Three-Shape menu ▲ and the Tic-Tac-Toe menu ●. The Three-Shape menu is specifically selected for the lower level option as it easily allows the menu to be broken into manageable bits. The menu itself can be cut along the dotted lines into strips of the same shape. Students can then be given the strip of square product choices for their use. Once they have chosen and submitted that product for grading, they can be given the circle strip, and finally the diamond strip. Because this type of menu is designed to become more advanced as students move through the shapes, teachers may choose to provide their lower level students with just the top two shapes and save the diamonds for enrichment.

Special Notes on the Use of These Menus

- The lower level menu ▲ is specifically designed for students who are lower level readers or for those with a more limited vocabulary. It is

meant to simply remind students of product options that have already been explained.

- The on-level menu ● asks students to use recycled materials to create their puppets. This does not mean only plastic and paper; instead, students should focus on using materials in new ways. It works well if a box is started for "recycled" contributions at the beginning of the school year. That way, students always have access to these types of materials.
- The lower level menu ▲ has students try to identify the shape (by sound alone) of a mystery object in a box assembled by the teacher. In order to create the mystery box, simply place an object (e.g., desk bell, stapler, paperclips) into a shoebox and tape it shut. Students can then use the box during center time or during menu time as one of their choices.

Time Frame

- 1–2 weeks—Students are given a menu as the unit is started. As the teacher presents lessons throughout the week, he or she should refer back to the menu options associated with that content. The teacher will go over all of the options for that content and have students select the activities they are most interested in completing. As teaching continues over the next week, activities are completed. For those students working on the Tic-Tac-Toe menu ●, the selected activities should make a column or row. The teacher may choose to dedicate a learning center to working on menu products or simply allow students time to work after other work is finished. When students complete this pattern, they will have completed one activity from each content area, learning style, or level of Bloom's revised taxonomy, depending on the design of the menu.
- 1 week—At the start of the unit, the teacher chooses the three activities he or she feels are most valuable for students. Stations can be set up in the classroom. These three activities are available for student choice throughout the week as regular instruction takes place.
- 1–2 days—The teacher chooses an activity from the menu to use with the entire class.

Suggested Forms

- All-purpose rubric

BASIC SHAPES

List and draw the shapes you will use on this menu here:

Directions: Pick a square. Circle it. Color in the square when you are done.

My shapes	Shapes around me	All the shapes
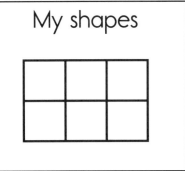		

Directions: Pick a circle. Circle it. Color in the circle when you are done.

3 circles,
4 squares,
1 triangle, and 2 stars

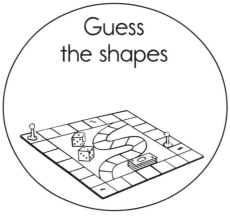

Guess
the shapes

Basic
shapes

Directions: Pick a diamond. Circle it. Color in the diamond when you are done.

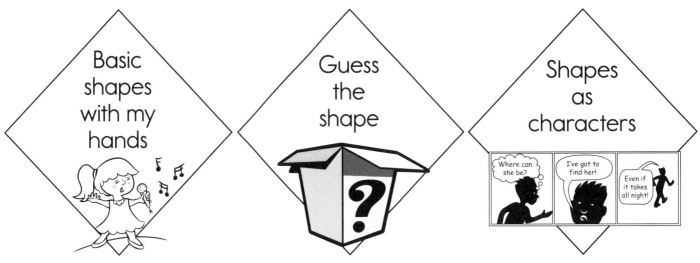

Basic
shapes
with my
hands

Guess
the
shape

Shapes
as
characters

BASIC SHAPES

Directions: Check the boxes you plan to complete. They should form a tic-tac-toe across or down. All activities must be completed by _____.

List and draw the shapes you will use on this menu here:

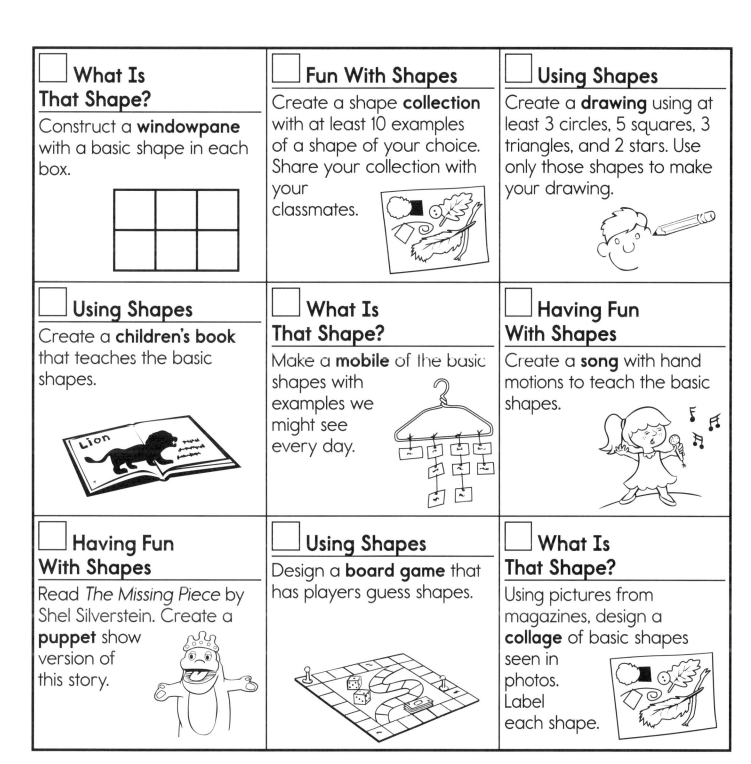

☐ **What Is That Shape?**

Construct a **windowpane** with a basic shape in each box.

☐ **Fun With Shapes**

Create a shape **collection** with at least 10 examples of a shape of your choice. Share your collection with your classmates.

☐ **Using Shapes**

Create a **drawing** using at least 3 circles, 5 squares, 3 triangles, and 2 stars. Use only those shapes to make your drawing.

☐ **Using Shapes**

Create a **children's book** that teaches the basic shapes.

☐ **What Is That Shape?**

Make a **mobile** of the basic shapes with examples we might see every day.

☐ **Having Fun With Shapes**

Create a **song** with hand motions to teach the basic shapes.

☐ **Having Fun With Shapes**

Read *The Missing Piece* by Shel Silverstein. Create a **puppet** show version of this story.

☐ **Using Shapes**

Design a **board game** that has players guess shapes.

☐ **What Is That Shape?**

Using pictures from magazines, design a **collage** of basic shapes seen in photos. Label each shape.

SPACE FIGURES

THREE-SHAPE MENU

Objectives Covered Through This Menu and These Activities

- Students will identify and compare various space figures including rectangular prisms, cubes, cylinders, cones, and spheres.

Materials Needed by Students for Completion

- Space figure blocks
- Socks (for puppets)
- Paper bags (for puppets)
- Recycled materials (for puppets)
- Space Figures Cube template
- Shoeboxes (for dioramas)
- Magazines (for collages)

Special Notes on the Modifications of These Menus

- These two Three-Shape menus have slightly different formats. The lower level menu ▲ has a dotted line with separate instructions for each section. This visually separates the page beyond just the different shapes. This also makes it easy for the teacher to cut the menu as needed based on the comfort level of the students when it comes to choice. If it is the first time choice is being introduced, the children may receive only the strip of square options. Then when they have finished, they can receive the circles and then the diamonds. After students are more accustomed to options, the menu might be cut just once after the circles, so students can select a square and a circle and submit them to the teacher. Then they can choose from the diamond strip they receive. The ultimate goal would be to work up to allowing students to have all nine options at once and not be overwhelmed. The on-level menu ● has one dotted line separating the diamonds from the rest of the menu, making the enrichment options easy to include or cut and distribute later at the teacher's discretion.

Special Notes on the Use of These Menus

- The lower level menu ▲ is specifically designed for students who are lower level readers or for those with a more limited vocabulary. It is meant to simply remind students of product options that have already been explained.
- These menus ask students to use recycled materials to create their puppets. This does not mean only plastic and paper; instead, students should focus on using materials in new ways. It works well if a box is started for "recycled" contributions at the beginning of the school year. That way, students always have access to these types of materials.

Time Frame

- 1–2 weeks—Students are given a menu as the unit is started. As the unit progresses throughout the week, students should refer back to the menu options associated with that content. The teacher will go over all of the options for that content and have students circle the items that represent the activities they are most interested in completing. As teaching continues over the next 1–2 weeks, shapes will be colored in as each activity is completed. The activities should be completed in such a way that students complete one from each shape group. When students complete this pattern, they will have completed one activity from each content area, learning style, or level of Bloom's revised taxonomy, depending on the design of the menu.
- 1–2 days—The teacher chooses an activity or product from an objective to use with the entire class during that lesson time.

Suggested Forms

- All-purpose rubric

SPACE FIGURES

Draw all of the space figures you need to use in this menu:

Directions: Pick a square. Circle it. Color in the square when you are done.

All of the figures above 	Singing about all of the space figures 	Labeling the shapes in the pictures 

Directions: Pick a circle. Circle it. Color in the circle when you are done.

Riddles for each of the shapes

2 space figures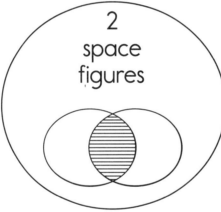

6 different space figures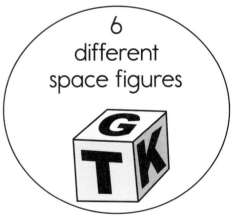

Directions: Pick a diamond. Circle it. Color in the diamond when you are done.

A space figure creature

The best space figure

A space figure animal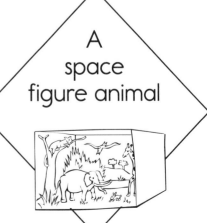

Name:_____ ●

SPACE FIGURES

Draw all of the space figures you need to use in this menu:

Directions: Pick a square. Circle it. Color in the square when you are done.

Make a space figure **flipbook,** with a flap for each of the space figures. 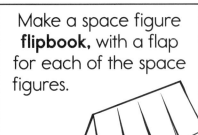	Write a **song** using all of the space figures listed above. 	Make a **collage** with pictures of objects with space figures. Label the pictures. 

Directions: Pick a circle. Circle it. Color in the circle when you are done.

Construct a **folded quiz book** with riddles for each of the 3-D shapes.

Make a **Venn diagram** to compare and contrast two space figures.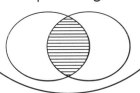

Create a **cube** with clues to six different space figures. Make your clues tricky!

- -

Directions: Pick a diamond. Circle it. Color in the diamond when you are done.

Use space figures to create a new creature. Make a **diorama** to show its surroundings. List all of the space figures you used to make the creature.

Design a space figure **puppet**. Have it talk about itself and explain why it is the best space figure of all.

Keep a space figure **diary**. Record every space figure you see for an entire day. Tell what each figure was and where you saw it.

SPACE FIGURES CUBE

Directions: List and number your space figures in the answer key. Write clues on each side of the cube so your classmates can guess what that space figure might be. Make your clues tricky to so your classmates have to really think about it! Use this pattern or create your own cube.

Answer Key:

Space Figure 1:

Space Figure 2:

Space Figure 3:

Space Figure 4:

Space Figure 5:

Space Figure 6:

Space Figure 1

Space Figure 2

Space Figure 3

Space Figure 4

Space Figure 5

Space Figure 6

READING GRAPHS

THREE-SHAPE MENU

Objectives Covered Through This Menu and These Activities

- Students will make predictions and draw conclusions based on graphs.
- Students will read bar, circle, and picture graphs.

Materials Needed by Students for Completion

- Poster board or large white paper
- Graph paper
- Blank index cards (for mobiles and trading cards ●)
- Coat hangers (for mobiles)
- String (for mobiles)
- Scrapbooking materials
- Newspapers and magazines (for scrapbooks)
- Materials for bulletin board display

Special Notes on the Modifications of These Menus

- These two Three-Shape menus have slightly different formats. The lower level menu ▲ has a dotted line with separate instructions for each section. This visually separates the page beyond just the different shapes. This also makes it easy for the teacher to cut the menu as needed based on the comfort level of the students when it comes to choice. If it is the first time choice is being introduced, the children may receive only the strip of square options. Then when they have finished, they can receive the circles and then the diamonds. After students are more accustomed to options, the menu might be cut just once after the circles, so students can select a square and a circle and submit them to the teacher. Then they can choose from the diamond strip they receive. The ultimate goal would be to work up to allowing students to have all nine options at once and not be overwhelmed. The on-level menu ● has one dotted line separating the diamonds from the rest of the menu, making the enrichment options easy to include or cut and distribute later at the teacher's discretion.

Special Notes on the Use of These Menus

- The lower level menu ▲ is specifically designed for students who are lower level readers or for those with a more limited vocabulary. It is meant to simply remind students of product options that have already been explained.
- These menus ● allow students to create a bulletin board display. Some classrooms may have only one bulletin board, so the teacher can divide the board into sections, or additional classroom wall or hall space can be sectioned off for the creation of these displays. Students can plan their displays based on the amount of space they are assigned.

Time Frame

- 1–2 weeks—Students are given a menu as the unit is started. As the unit progresses throughout the week, students should refer back to the menu options associated with that content. The teacher will go over all of the options for that content and have students circle the items that represent the activities they are most interested in completing. As teaching continues over the next 1–2 weeks, shapes will be colored in as each activity is completed. The activities should be completed in such a way that students complete one from each shape group. When students complete this pattern, they will have completed one activity from each content area, learning style, or level of Bloom's revised taxonomy, depending on the design of the menu.
- 1–2 days—The teacher chooses an activity or product from an objective to use with the entire class during that lesson time.

Suggested Forms

- All-purpose rubric
- Free-choice proposal form (if appropriate for content and level of students)

READING GRAPHS

Directions: Pick a square. Circle it. Color in the square when you are done.

Types of graphs	Different types of graphs	3 different graphs
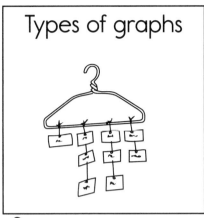	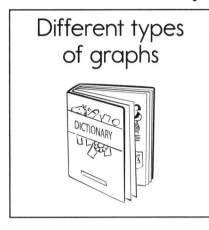	

✂ -

Directions: Pick a circle. Circle it. Color in the circle when you are done.

Explaining a graph

The sky is blue today. I see a boat on the lake and a man fishing. There is a bird singing in the tree outside my window. I will soon eat breakfast and go for a bike ride with my friend Julie. It is a good day.

2 sentences about each graph

Different types of graphs and how to read them

✂ -

Directions: Pick a diamond. Circle it. Color in the diamond when you are done.

The hardest graph

Easy-to-read and understand graphs

Different types of graphs

READING GRAPHS

Directions: Pick a square. Circle it. Color in the square when you are done.

Create a **mobile** for the different types of graphs we are studying. 	Design a **windowpane** to show the different types of graphs. 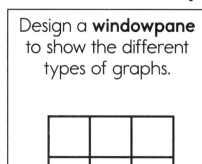	Make a set of **trading cards** for the different types of graphs and what each one shows. 

Directions: Pick a circle. Circle it. Color in the circle when you are done.

Create an **acrostic** for the name of one of the types of graphs. Use each letter of the word to describe how to use the graph.
Write the word
Oval letters
Remember the word
Draw a picture

Design a **scrapbook** of graphs you find in newspapers or magazines. Write two sentences about each graph.

Make a **Venn diagram** to compare and contrast 2 types of graphs and what they show.
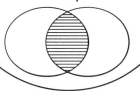

- -

Directions: Pick a diamond. Circle it. Color in the diamond when you are done.

Develop a **poster** for the graph you think is the hardest to read. Write a paragraph on the back of the poster that explains why you think this.

Create a **bulletin board display** that shares examples of each type of graph we are studying.

Free

Free choice— Submit a proposal form to your teacher for a product of your choice.

PERIMETER

GIVE ME 5 MENU

Objectives Covered Through This Menu and These Activities

- Students will measure and calculate the perimeter of various regular and irregular objects.
- Students will understand that perimeter is the distance around an object.

Materials Needed by Students for Completion

- Poster board or large white paper
- Large blank or lined index cards (for instruction cards)
- Materials for bulletin board ●
- Map of your state ●
- Materials for class game (folders, colored cards, etc.) ●

Special Notes on the Modifications of These Menus

- Because the Give Me 5 menu is a point-based menu, it is easy to modify by changing the point goal for those students for whom a goal of 5 may be too much. Lowering the goal on each menu by 1 (or 2) may be more appropriate for some students. Students can color in the "extra" graphics on the bottom of the menu so that the colored graphics match the original goal of 5 points.

Special Notes on the Use of These Menus

- The lower level menu ▲ is specifically designed for students who are lower level readers or for those with a more limited vocabulary. It is meant to simply remind students of product options that have already been explained.
- The on-level menu ● allows students to create a bulletin board display. Some classrooms may have only one bulletin board, so the teacher can divide the board into sections, or additional classroom wall or hall space can be sectioned off for the creation of these displays. Students can plan their displays based on the amount of space they are assigned.

Time Frame

- 1–3 days—Students are given a menu as the unit is started, and the teacher discusses all of the product options on the menu. As the different options are discussed, students color the graphic for each option that represents the activity they are most interested in completing so they meet their goal of 5 points. In this menu, that would imply students complete either two products (a 2-point and a 3-point) or one 5-point product. As students complete products, they will color the corresponding graphics along the bottom of the menu so they can track their progress toward their 5-point goal. As the lessons progress throughout the week, the teacher and students refer back to the menu options associated with the content being taught. The teacher may choose to dedicate a learning center to working on menu products or simply allow students time to work after other work is finished.
- 1 day—The teacher chooses an activity or product from the menu to use with the entire class.

Suggested Forms

- All-purpose rubric

PERIMETER

Directions: Choose activities from the menu below. The activities must total 5. Color or circle the picture next to each choice to show which activities you will complete. Color the rulers along the bottom as you complete your activities to reach 5! All activities must be completed by _____.

2  Measuring the perimeter of different shapes

 Easiest way to measure perimeter

3 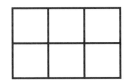 Perimeter of 10 regular objects

 Perimeter of 3 irregularly shaped objects

5  At least 8 things with a perimeter of 10 cm

 Calculating your state's perimeter

PERIMETER

Directions: Choose activities from the menu below. The activities must total 5. Color or circle the picture next to each choice to show which activities you will complete. Color the rulers along the bottom as you complete your activities to reach 5! All activities must be completed by _____.

2

Write an **instruction card** that tells how to measure the perimeter of different shapes.

Create a **flipbook** of shapes. Draw the shape on the front, and write how to find the perimeter on the inside.

3

Find 3 objects in the room with perimeters of about 50 cm, 72 cm, and 2 meters. Make a **list** of all of the items you measured before you found 3 with these measurements.

Choose an irregularly shaped figure in your classroom. Develop a plan for calculating the perimeter, and then find the perimeter. Show your results in a **drawing**.

5

Create a **class game** that has your classmates practicing their ability to measure perimeter. Be sure to include an answer key.

Scale is used on maps to show large distances. Using a map of your state, calculate its perimeter. Design a **bulletin board** display that shows step-by-step how to do the calculations.

CHAPTER 8

Measurement Menus

CALENDAR

MEAL MENU

Objectives Covered Through This Menu and These Activities

- Students will name the months of the year in order.
- Students will share activities done in each month.
- Students will investigate the origins of the names of our months (optional).

Materials Needed by Students for Completion

- Poster board or large white paper
- Blank index cards (for mobiles)
- Coat hangers (for mobiles)
- String (for mobiles)
- Graph paper or Internet access (for crossword puzzle) ●
- Socks (for puppets) ▲
- Paper bags (for puppets) ▲
- Recycled materials (for puppets ▲ and models ●)
- Shoeboxes (for dioramas) ▲
- Magazines (for collages)
- Microsoft PowerPoint or other slideshow software ●

Special Notes on the Modifications of These Menus

- The Meal menu format has a design feature that makes it easy to reduce the number of choices students face at one time. Students can be given the left side (breakfast and lunch, or lower levels of thinking) as their first options. After these two meal products have been completed, students can then receive the right side (dinner and dessert, or higher levels of thinking and enrichment options). After becoming accustomed to the amount of choice, students can then get the entire meal menu at once.

Special Notes on the Use of These Menus

- The lower level menu ▲ is specifically designed for students who are lower level readers or for those with a more limited vocabulary. It is

meant to simply remind students of product options that have already been explained.

- These menus ask students to use recycled materials to create their puppets ▲ and models ●. This does not mean only plastic and paper; instead, students should focus on using materials in new ways. It works well if a box is started for "recycled" contributions at the beginning of the school year. That way, students always have access to these types of materials.

Time Frame

- 1 week—Students are given a menu as the unit is started. As the unit progresses throughout the week, students should refer back to the menu options associated with that content. The teacher will go over all of the options for that content and have students color or circle the graphic for each option that represents the activity they are most interested in completing. As teaching continues, the activities chosen and completed should create a full day's meal, with a breakfast, a lunch, a dinner, and an optional dessert. The teacher may choose to dedicate a learning center to working on menu products or simply allow students times to work after other work is finished. When students complete the menu with this expectation, they have completed one activity from each content area, learning style, or level of Bloom's revised taxonomy, depending on the design of the menu.
- 1–2 days—The teacher chooses an activity or product from an objective to use with the entire class during that lesson time.

Suggested Forms

- All-purpose rubric
- Free-choice proposal form (if appropriate for content and level of students)

CALENDAR

Directions: Choose one activity for breakfast and lunch.

Breakfast

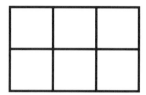

All of the months of the year

Pictures for each month

The seasons and the months for each season

Lunch

All of the important dates in a year

My favorite month

Activities during my favorite month

Directions: Choose one activity for dinner. After you are done with your dinner, you may do a dessert.

Dinner

 All of the months of the year

 My own calendar

 One whole week

Dessert

 The best month

 The perfect day in December

CALENDAR

Directions: Choose one activity for breakfast and lunch.

Breakfast

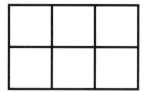

Design a **windowpane** with 12 squares. Write one month in each square, and draw a picture for each one.

Make a **mobile** that includes each season, the months in that season, and what you like do during each.

Create a **collage** with pictures for each month of the year. Label the pictures with the months.

Lunch

Design your own calendar using pictures or **drawings**. Include all of the months.

Record all of the important dates for one year onto a blank calendar; include national dates and family dates. Glue your calendar onto a **poster**.

Perform a **song** about your favorite month. Be sure to tell what you like to do during that month.

Directions: Choose one activity for dinner. After you are done with your dinner, you may do a dessert.

Dinner

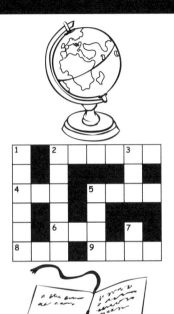

Here is a riddle for you to solve: How many months have 28 days? Find the correct answer and design a **model** to prove your answer is correct.

Create a **crossword puzzle** with questions about the months of the year and the calendar.

Keep a **diary** every day for a week. Be sure to record what day it is each day and what you did that was special!

Dessert

Research the history of the names of our months. Make a **PowerPoint presentation** to share the information.

Write a **play** about the month that you like the best. Include what you like to do during that month and why it is your favorite.

TEMPERATURE

PICK 3 MENU ▲ AND TARGET-BASED LIST MENU ●

Objectives Covered Through This Menu and These Activities

- Students will read temperature using a thermometer.
- Students will distinguish between temperatures that seem hot and cold.
- Students will share how they measure and use temperatures in their daily lives.

Materials Needed by Students for Completion

- Poster board or large white paper
- Large blank or lined index cards (for instruction cards) ●
- Blank index cards (for concentration cards, trading cards, and mobiles)
- Coat hangers (for mobiles)
- String (for mobiles)
- Scrapbooking materials ●
- Socks (for puppets)
- Paper bags (for puppets)
- Recycled materials (for puppets)
- Shoeboxes (for dioramas)
- Thermometers
- Materials for board games (folders, colored cards, etc.)

Special Notes on the Modifications of These Menus

- This topic has two different menu formats: the Pick 3 menu ▲ and the Target-Based List menu ●. Although the activities are similar, some students may be overwhelmed by the design of the Target-Based List menu. The Pick 3 menu visually distinguishes the options separately using boxes and can be modified further by dividing the page into three sections, in which the students select one option from each section.

Special Notes on the Use of These Menus

- The lower level menu ▲ is specifically designed for students who are lower level readers or for those with a more limited vocabulary. It is

meant to simply remind students of product options that have already been explained.

- These menus ask students to use recycled materials to create their puppets. This does not mean only plastic and paper; instead, students should focus on using materials in new ways. It works well if a box is started for "recycled" contributions at the beginning of the school year. That way, students always have access to these types of materials.

Time Frame

- 1–2 weeks—Students are given a menu as the unit is started and the guidelines and target number of products are discussed. The Target-Based List menu ● has an open blank at the top so teachers can designate their own target values based on time and knowledge of the students. A target number of 3 is a good place to begin, and teachers can adjust this based on student expertise. There is also an opportunity for extra credit if the teacher would like to use another target number. Because these menus cover one topic in depth, the teacher will go over all of the options on the menus and have students circle or place check marks in the boxes next to the activities they are most interested in completing. If students are using the Target-Based List menu ●, teachers will also need to set aside a few moments to sign the agreement at the bottom of the page with each student; this is not necessary with the Pick 3 menu ▲. As instruction continues, activities are completed by students and submitted for grading. The teacher may choose to dedicate a learning center to working on menu products or simply allow students time to work after other work is finished.
- 1–2 days—The teacher chooses an activity or product from an objective to use with the entire class during that lesson time.

Suggested Forms

- All-purpose rubric
- Free-choice proposal form (if appropriate for content and level of students)

TEMPERATURE

Directions: Circle three activities you would like to do. Color in the square after you are finished.

Reading thermometers 	5 different temperatures and what you like to do 	Daily temperatures for a week 

Using temperature readings
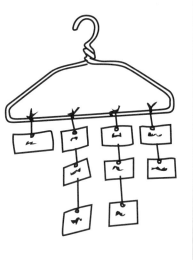

Matching temperatures with thermometers

Temperature and our daily lives

Knowing the temperature

My favorite temperature and activities

Using and reading a thermometer

Name:_____ ●

TEMPERATURE

Directions:

1. You may complete as many of the activities listed as you can within the time period.
2. You may choose any combination of activities. Your goal is to complete _____ activities.
3. You may be as creative as you like within the guidelines listed below.
4. You must share your plan with your teacher by _____.

Plan to Do	Activity to Complete	Completed
	Pretend you are a Fahrenheit thermometer. Write an **instruction card** that explains how to find your temperature.	
	Keep a **diary** of the daily temperatures for a week.	
	Design a set of **concentration cards** that matches temperatures with their readings on thermometers.	
	Create a set of **trading cards** with 10 different temperatures and what you like to do when they are the outside temperatures.	
	Design a thermometer **puppet**. Use your puppet to tell how temperature is important in our daily lives.	
	Create a **scrapbook** that has a temperature on the top of each page and pictures of what you like to do on days with that temperature.	
	Develop a **board game** in which players practice reading thermometers.	
	When people cook or bake, they use various temperatures. Make a **drawing** that shows the cooking temperatures of different foods. Be sure to use different temperatures!	
	Design a **mobile** showing the different ways that people use temperature readings.	
	Free choice—Submit a proposal form to your teacher for a product of your choice.	
	Total number of activities you are planning to complete:	Total number of activities completed:

I am planning to complete ____ activities.

Teacher's initials _____ Student's signature _____

TIME

THREE-SHAPE MENU ▲
AND TIC-TAC-TOE MENU ●

Objectives Covered Through This Menu and These Activities

- Students will tell time using an analog clock.
- Students will track and predict elapsed time.

Materials Needed by Students for Completion

- Poster board or large white paper
- Blank index cards (for concentration cards)
- Paper bags (for puppets) ●
- Socks (for puppets) ●
- Recycled materials (for puppets) ●
- Graph paper or Internet access (for crossword puzzle) ●
- Magazines (for collages) ▲
- Materials for board games (folders, colored cards, etc.)
- Scrapbooking materials

Special Notes on the Modifications of These Menus

- This topic has two different menu formats: the Three-Shape menu ▲ and the Tic-Tac-Toe menu ●. The Three-Shape menu is specifically selected for the lower level option as it easily allows the menu to be broken into manageable bits. The menu itself can be cut along the dotted lines into strips of the same shape. Students can then be given the strip of square product choices for their use. Once they have chosen and submitted that product for grading, they can be given the circle strip, and finally the diamond strip. Because this type of menu is designed to become more advanced as students move through the shapes, teachers may choose to provide their lower level students with just the top two shapes and save the diamonds for enrichment.

Special Notes on the Use of These Menus

- The lower level menu ▲ is specifically designed for students who are lower level readers or for those with a more limited vocabulary. It is

meant to simply remind students of product options that have already been explained.

- The lower level menu ▲ asks students to use recycled materials to create their puppets. This does not mean only plastic and paper; instead, students should focus on using materials in new ways. It works well if a box is started for "recycled" contributions at the beginning of the school year. That way, students always have access to these types of materials.

Time Frame

- 1–2 weeks—Students are given a menu as the unit is started. As the teacher presents lessons throughout the week, he or she should refer back to the menu options associated with that content. The teacher will go over all of the options for that content and have students select the activities they are most interested in completing. As teaching continues over the next week, activities are completed. For those students working on the Tic-Tac-Toe menu ●, the selected activities should make a column or row. The teacher may choose to dedicate a learning center to working on menu products or simply allow students time to work after other work is finished. When students complete this pattern, they will have completed one activity from each content area, learning style, or level of Bloom's revised taxonomy, depending on the design of the menu.
- 1 week—At the start of the unit, the teacher chooses the three activities he or she feels are most valuable for students. Stations can be set up in the classroom. These three activities are available for student choice throughout the week as regular instruction takes place.
- 1–2 days—The teacher chooses an activity from the menu to use with the entire class.

Suggested Forms

- All-purpose rubric
- Free-choice proposal form (if appropriate for content and level of students)

TIME

Directions: Pick a square. Circle it. Color in the square when you are done.

Important times	How to tell time	Ways adults use time
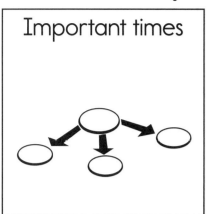		

Directions: Pick a circle. Circle it. Color in the circle when you are done.

Important words used in telling time

Telling time using clocks

Matching times with clocks

Directions: Pick a diamond. Circle it. Color in the diamond when you are done.

Schedule for your perfect day

Activities for 5 minutes or less, 15–30 minutes, and an hour

Important times in your day

TIME

Directions: Check the boxes you plan to complete. They should form a tic-tac-toe across or down. All activities must be completed by _____.

☐ **Why Time Is Important** Perform a **play** about a person who doesn't know how to tell time and how this affects his or her life.	☐ **Telling Time** Make a **crossword puzzle** in which the clues are clocks and the answers are the correct times on the clocks. 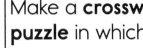	☐ **Passing Time** Make a **scrapbook** of activities that can be done in 5 minutes or less, 15–30 minutes, and an hour.
☐ **Passing Time** Create a set of **concentration cards** where players match two items with the amount of time passing between them.	☐ **Free Choice** (Fill out your proposal form before beginning the free choice!)	☐ **Telling Time** There are different ways to say the same time. Design a **windowpane** telling all of the ways you could express 2:35.
☐ **Telling Time** Create a **board game** using clock drawings so your classmates can practice telling time. 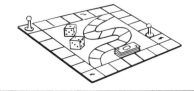	☐ **Passing Time** Develop a schedule for your perfect day that includes what you would do at certain times and how much time would be spent on each activity. Put your schedule on a **poster**.	☐ **Why Time Is Important** Ask at least 5 adults why time is important. Make a **mind map** to share what you discovered.

—

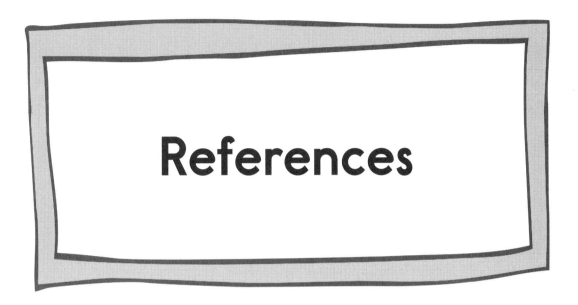

References

Anderson, L. W., & Krathwohl, D. R. (Eds.). (2001). *A taxonomy for learning, teaching, and assessing: A revision of Bloom's taxonomy of educational objectives.* New York, NY: Allyn & Bacon.

Cipani, E. (1995). Inclusive education: What do we know and what do we still have to learn? *Exceptional Children, 61,* 498 500.

Cusumano, C., & Mueller, J. (2007). How differentiated instruction helps struggling students. *Educational Leadership, 36*(4), 8–10

Mercer, C. D., Lane, H. B., Jordan, L., Allsopp, D. H., & Eisele, M. R. (1996). Empowering teachers and students with instructional choices in inclusive settings. *Remedial and Special Education, 17,* 226–236.

Shevin, M., & Klein, N. (2004). The importance of choice-making skills for students with severe disabilities. *Research & Practice for Persons With Severe Disabilities, 29,* 161–168.

Silverstein, S. (1976). *The missing piece.* New York, NY: Harper and Row.

Note

The articles by Cipani (1995), Cusumano and Mueller (2007), and Shevin and Klein (2004) were used to gather background information on inclusion, differentiated instruction, and choice for this book.

About the Author

After teaching science for more than 15 years, both overseas and in the U.S., **Laurie E. Westphal** now works as an independent gifted education and science consultant nationwide. She enjoys developing and presenting staff development on differentiation for various districts and conferences, working with teachers to assist them in planning and developing lessons to meet the needs of all students. Laurie currently resides in Houston, TX, and has made it her goal to convert as many teachers as she can to the differentiated lifestyle in the classroom and share her vision for real-world, product-based lessons that help all students become critical thinkers and effective problem solvers.

If you are interested in having Laurie speak at your next staff development day or conference, please visit her website, http://www.giftedconsultant.com, for additional information.

Additional Titles by the Author

Laurie E. Westphal has written many books on using differentiation strategies in the classroom, providing teachers of grades K–8 with creative, engaging, ready-to-use resources. Among them are:

Differentiating Instruction With Menus, Grades K–2
(Math, Language Arts, Science, and Social Studies volumes available)

Differentiating Instruction With Menus, Grades 3–5
(Math, Language Arts, Science, and Social Studies volumes available)

Differentiating Instruction With Menus, Grades 6–8
(Math, Language Arts, Science, and Social Studies volumes available)

Differentiating Instruction With Menus for the Inclusive Classroom, Grades K–2
(Math, Language Arts, Science, and Social Studies volumes available)

Differentiating Instruction With Menus for the Inclusive Classroom, Grades 3–5
(Math, Language Arts, Science, and Social Studies volumes available)

Differentiating Instruction With Menus for the Inclusive Classroom, Grades 6–8
(Math, Language Arts, Science, and Social Studies volumes available)

**For a current listing of Laurie's books, please visit
Prufrock Press at http://www.prufrock.com.**